Teachers

Originally published in 1994, Teachers: Constructing a Future is designed for teachers, as well as those interested in the future of schooling and education. The book draws on sociological analysis, philosophical insights and aspects of political economy to examine the changing and developing role of teachers in the context of the current transformation of western capitalism. It considers the historical growth of teaching as a profession and as a political force, and indicates that economic rationalism has been effectively employed to elevate the instrumental role of schooling in society, and consequentially to devalue the professional and political nature of teaching.

Teachers

Constructing the Future

by Kevin Harris

Routledge
Taylor & Francis Group

First published in 1994
by The Falmer Press.

This edition first published in 2018 by Routledge
2 Park Square, Milton Park, Abingdon, Oxon, OX14 4RN
and by Routledge
711 Third Avenue, New York, NY 10017

Routledge is an imprint of the Taylor & Francis Group, an informa business

Publisher's Note
The publisher has gone to great lengths to ensure the quality of this reprint but points out that some imperfections in the original copies may be apparent.

Disclaimer
The publisher has made every effort to trace copyright holders and welcomes correspondence from those they have been unable to contact.

A Library of Congress record exists under LCCN: 93021333

ISBN 13: 978-0-8153-6260-9 (hbk)
ISBN 13: 978-1-351-11183-6 (ebk)
ISBN 13: 978-0-8153-6261-6 (pbk)

Teachers: Constructing the Future

Agitators are a set of interfering, meddling people, who come down to some perfectly contented class of the community and sow the seeds of discontent among them. That is the reason why agitators are so absolutely necessary. Without them, in our incomplete state, there would be no advance towards civilisation.

Oscar Wilde

One of the most important characteristics of any group that is developing towards dominance is its struggle to assimilate and to conquer 'ideologically' the traditional intellectuals, but this assimilation and conquest is made quicker and more efficacious the more the group in question succeeds in simultaneously elaborating its own organic intellectuals.

A human mass does not 'distinguish' itself, does not become independent in its own right without, in the widest sense, organising itself; and there is no organization without intellectuals, that is without organizers and leaders, in other words without the theoretic aspect of the theory-practice nexus being distinguished concretely by the existence of a group of people 'specialised' in conceptual and philosophical elaboration of ideas.

Antonio Gramsci

Teachers:
Constructing the Future

Kevin Harris

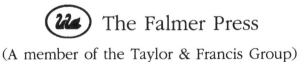 The Falmer Press

(A member of the Taylor & Francis Group)
London • Washington, D.C.

UK	The Falmer Press, 4 John Street, London WC1N 2ET
USA	The Falmer Press, Taylor & Francis Inc., 1900 Frost Road, Suite 101, Bristol, PA 19007

First published 1994

A catalogue record for this book is available from the British Library

Library of Congress Cataloging-in-Publication Data are available on request

ISBN 075070 300 8 cased
ISBN 075070 301 6 paper

Jacket design by Caroline Archer

Typeset in 11/13 pt Garamond
by Graphicraft Typesetters Ltd., Hong Kong.

Contents

Note on the Text

This book has been written for trainee teachers, practising teachers and teachers of teachers, as well as for anyone else interested in the future of schooling and education. I have attempted to keep the argument as rigorous as it need be in order that it may be cogent and compelling without seeking recourse to polemics, but at the same time I have sought to divest the book as far as possible of unnecessary 'academic' trappings so that its central argument is not held up or diverted by displays of professional scholarship. To those ends I have, on the one hand, not shied away from philosophical and sociological argument which, as my experience continually affirms, teachers are well at home with; but I have, on the other hand, kept notes to a minimum and I have placed references within the text only where either quotations or precise and direct sources need to be acknowledged. Extensive direction to further reading is given in the bibliography.

Earlier versions of some of the arguments in this book have been worked through in papers of mine which previously appeared in *Education Research and Perspectives*, the *New Zealand Journal of Educational Studies* and the *Journal of Philosophy of Education*. I wish to thank the editors of those journals for permission to reuse and develop any material which they originally published.

The title of the book, and much else concerning it, was inspired by Ivan Snook, Professor of Education at Massey University, New Zealand, who has been a constant champion of teachers and teacher-professionalism. The presentation of the book owes much to Maureen Harris who assisted in transferring many versions of scrawled text to discs and legible hard copy. The book itself is for my child, David, who has just begun his schooling, and for the teachers who will teach him, his peers and their progeny.

Kevin Harris
Macquarie University
September 1993

Preface

In 1885 teachers were trained in classrooms to perform the specific functions of instruction and control. Over the course of the next century they had become highly educated professionals. By 1985, while still continuing with classroom instruction and control, teachers had become a body of people who were highly knowledgeable with regard to educational theory and practice, sociology, social theory, child psychology, learning theory and so on. They had become experts in their subject content; and they had won the right, as a professional body, to be centrally involved in the determination and development of curriculum content, schooling practices and educational policy in general.

By 1995 they are likely to have lost, in a single decade, most of the gains made in the preceding century.

It is society as a whole, however, that will be the bigger loser. As Grace (1988) and Snook (1989) have argued respectively, the ability of people to participate meaningfully in a democratic social context is dependent to a significant extent upon the quality of education in a society, which is in turn dependent upon the quality of the teachers within the education system.

This book examines the role of schools, and particularly that of teachers, in social reconstruction. It argues that in today's circumstances we would do well to find ways of going against prevailing trends by seeking to produce better educated and more highly professionalized teachers. Further, and more significantly, it argues that such teachers should have greater control of the process and content of schooling, and that they should take a vanguard role in social reconstruction directed towards promoting increased autonomy and real democratic participation of the citizenry.

Reprofessionalizing and Politicizing Teachers

Teacher-professionalism in the Western world reached its heights around the mid-1980s. Since then there have been varied but interconnected moves to change the role and nature of teaching. Almost all of these, many of which shall be detailed later, have to do with eroding teachers' autonomy and control and can be seen as part of a process of de-professionalization, which is itself part of a larger process that recent analyses of the job of schoolteaching have pointed overwhelmingly to, and which is now commonly referred to as proletarianization.

'Proletarianization' has both a technical sense and a more general sense. In its technical sense proletarianization centres around deskilling and devaluing labour, and refers specifically to the economic process of devaluation of labour power from skilled to average levels.

This is the sense which I followed and detailed when I argued over a decade ago (Harris, 1982) that teaching was already in the process of becoming deskilled and devalued as labour power, and that it would continue in that direction. Teachers, I argued, could expect to lose economic ground, as well as political and ideological social status. They could expect to do more controlling and less curricular instructing for their money, and in the process find their instruction function deskilled. I suggested also that they were likely, globally, to lose aspects of control over the content they teach and over the general rather than local conditions under which they work; that they would increasingly assume management functions, with the relevant skills being devalued as labour power; and that they would decreasingly instruct, again with the relevant skills becoming devalued as labour power.

In this context I noted that, while teachers' economic, political and ideological privileges faced gradual erosion as teaching itself moved further away from instructional activities and more towards the function of control and management, teachers would not completely lose these privileges. Rather, the basis for maintaining them would change. My prediction at the beginning of the 1980s (*ibid*) was that:

> Economic privilege will be bestowed for the work of political and ideological control; and in order to maintain this privilege teachers will experience a new and increased intensity of work, and a new type of work concerned less with direct instruction and more with direct administration and control, itself subject to more administration and control from above. (p. 137)

That teachers have become, and are going to become, even more accountable in crude cost-benefit terms, and that they will have to perform increased and changing tasks to maintain marginal economic privilege, appears to have been borne out in recent developments regarding the structure and provision of schooling in at least the UK, the USA, Canada, New Zealand and Australia. In the last decade it has been the massive tendency for teachers, from early childhood to university level, to do less instructing and more administrative or management-type control work; and to do this for a generally decreasing marginal salary advantage over that paid for average labour power, even though teachers' actual wages have been rising. This process will in all likelihood accelerate as the current moves towards local management of schooling gain pace and as particular principles of economic and technocratic rationalism are increasingly applied to schooling.

The increasing proletarianization of teachers in the broader but no less useful sense of loss of professional control, autonomy and social status, has also been thoroughly documented. For instance, in considering the impact of recent educational developments in New Zealand following from major Reports such as *Administering for Excellence* (Picot, 1988) and *Tomorrow's Schools* (Lange, 1988), Marshall and Peters (1990) note:

> These 'reforms' have effectively cut off the input of teachers into the curriculum and disempowered them in matters of salary and conditions of work, through new institutional structures and conditions of employment which were not negotiated but, essentially, imposed. In these 'reforms' the language of quality, excellence, choice and devolution to the community looms large. But the areas over which teachers can exercise their professional expertise have been seriously reduced. It is hardly surprising that already questions are being asked in the new ministry about the need for the professional preparation of teachers. (p. 163)

In Australia too current rounds of award restructuring are contributing disturbingly to the deprofessionalization of groups such as teachers. Within a larger process of adopting forms and processes of corporate managerialism, professionals such as teachers are being redefined as straight-out contracted employees subject to direct management, and are becoming positioned in such a way that their expertise and professional knowledge is decreasingly called upon with regard to decision-making in areas central to the needs and requirements of those whom they teach and serve. Teachers are having to leave decision-making in areas such as curriculum and educational goals and purposes to others, and instead become efficient managers of the human and financial resources in their schools, while their skill and worth as teachers is also now tending to be measured in terms of effective management. Michael Apple has recently reported a virtual limiting case of the managerial control of teachers in the USA — namely the growing practice of States legislating to mandate programs of competency testing for teachers. Apple (1986a) sees this as a clear instance 'of a considerably larger movement in which teachers are losing autonomy and in which their control of their skills and knowledge and of curricular and teaching policies and practices are being eviscerated' (p. 168).

Aronowitz and Giroux (1985) report more broadly on this movement. They generally endorse public criticisms of contemporary American schooling for failing 'to prepare students to think critically and creatively with regard to developing the sophisticated literacy skills necessary to make informed and effective choices about the worlds of work, politics, culture, personal relationships, and the economy' (p. 23); but they note that commonly proposed reforms relating to excellence and creative scholarship 'ignore the intelligence, judgment, and experience that teachers might bring to bear on such issues', and tend to be 'accompanied by policy suggestions that further erode the power teachers have over the conditions of their work while simultaneously proposing that administrators and teachers look outside of their schools for improvements and needed reforms' (*ibid*).

Aronowitz and Giroux argue that such proposals, along with the broader prevailing logic of technocratic rationality and pedagogical instrumentality, serve to remove teachers from critical participation in the production and evaluation of school curricula. They note also, as have many others, the 'reformist' tendency to reduce teachers to the status of low-level employees or civil servants receiving and implementing the dictates, objectives and goals of others situated within the upper levels of either the school or state bureaucracies. Aronowitz and Giroux bitterly decry what they perceive to be a developing trend towards 'the disempowerment of teachers at all levels of education' (p. 24), increasing public failure to recognize 'the central role that teachers must play in any viable attempt to revitalize the public schools' (pp. 23–4), and any tendency to reduce teacher autonomy in the development and planning of curricula.

As it turns out, varied cases for 'disempowering' teachers, lessening their autonomy and control, and devaluing their role in the determination of curriculum content and educational aims, can be found emanating from virtually all parts of the political and theoretic spectrum. For a number of reasons (some of which I shall detail later), discourse surrounding the role of the teacher has tended recently to promote a particular form of disempowerment of teachers, which I would characterize as 'subdued agency'. In starting either from a pessimistic view about the potential ineffectiveness of teachers to promote social change (a view ironically spawned by both correspondence and resistance theories of schooling), or from a moral concern over whether teachers have the right to manipulate other people and impose their goals on them, or from a political concern that those targetted for change might have no desire (or need) to be meddled with, or even from simply eschewing conflict theories of the state, this discourse has moved generally towards embracing the language of 'consensus'. It has cast the teacher not as the deliberate promoter of particular ends, but rather as one who lays out options without favour, and who facilitates the process of choice among available options within a context seeking, if not total consensus, then at least a form of social harmony. Disturbingly, some of the proposals advocated, such as that teachers be non-directive and instead key into pupils' cultural forms, or that policy and curriculum be taken out of teachers' hands and given to governments (through the establishment of bodies such as Boards of Studies and/or through the centralized development of National Curricula) are now emanating from both liberal and social-democratic sources, and are unwittingly or otherwise tending to support rather than oppose crude New Right positions.

This is not to say, however, that there does not also exist a considerable literature promoting teacher empowerment and teacher-control in schools. The problem here is that that side of the debate has been largely appropriated by economic rationalism. In this context the role of teachers has been repoliticized — away from broader concerns with determining curricula, formulating educational goals and promoting social reconstruction and towards the realm of efficient school management within an educational market-place; and among those favouring economic rationalism there are many who consider current initiatives such as the moves towards local management of schooling and school-based teacher education to be not proletarianization but rather part of a process of furthering the professionalism of teachers.

It is this restructuring, redefinition and repoliticizing of teaching that I believe needs to be particularly opposed. It is not that, provided certain other conditions prevail, I have anything against teachers managing schools or assisting with the pre- and in-service education of their co-professionals. In certain contexts those could be excellent things. Under present circumstances, however, redefinition of the job of teaching under titles and practices of award restructuring and local management of schooling has established a practical context of disempowerment and deprofessionalization within a rhetorical context of empowerment. The present history of teachers in much of the Western world has become one of decreased status and control with relation to educational issues, loss of autonomy, worsening of conditions, loss of purpose and direction, destruction of health, increased anxiety and depression, lowering of morale, and, despite a continued proliferation of policy rhetoric to the contrary, subjugation to increasing government and other external controls of schooling and curricula. The initiatives currently being imposed on teachers are serving, at one and the same time, to reduce the professional knowledge and critical scholarship which teachers bring to their work, and to decrease the political impact that teachers might bring to bear through their instructional activities.

I would want to see that situation changed. But I do not particularly want to argue for or against specific substantive points like local management of schooling here. They are certainly important; but while debate focuses on such issues more central matters of principle can easily get lost or be pushed out of court, and it is quite possible that in the resolution of details certain larger principles can be rendered first unproblematic and finally irrelevant. For instance, debates over the composition of School Councils can easily render unproblematic the prior issue of whether there ought to be School Councils in the first place. This being the case, and given that there is a related prior and larger issue tied up with the professionalism of teachers and their political role in society, I shall turn towards the broader concern of attempting to defend teaching against the threat of increasing impotency with regard to both determination of policy and social reconstruction.

A defence of teaching might be content to make a plea for maintaining the state of affairs reached in the mid-1980s; but I shall not be easily content. In a period of rapidly increasing proletarianization of teachers and at a time of what I consider to be extreme threat, in which teachers (as Aronowitz and Giroux hinted at) are commonly being portrayed as part of the problem with contemporary schooling rather than being viewed in terms of their potential to combat existing ills, there seems to be good reason to promote an extension of both teacher-professionalism and the political role of teaching, rather than employ a defensive strategy aimed at minimizing losses.

Schools are powerful agents in the process of consciousness formation and establishing hegemony, and in the present circumstances they are caught up actively in what Whitty (1992) and others have called the 'grand narrative' of the market (p. 22). Apple (1992a) has noted that 'the results of this "narrative" are visible every day in the destruction of our communities and environment . . . in the faces and bodies of our children, who see the future and turn away' (p. 27). Teachers educated in a particular way could be well qualified and well placed to help future generations construct a future worth looking towards. In what follows I shall argue that teachers can be sufficiently well placed to operate counter-hegemonically; and that in the contemporary context they should take an informed counter-hegemonic political-epistemological stance from which to control the educational purposes of their schools, and to direct those purposes towards the end of rational social reconstruction. Basically, I shall put a case for teachers to be counted among the intellectual vanguard in social reconstruction, and I shall make a call for teachers to take a prominent and active role in constructing the future.

Chapter 1

The Dead Hand of the Past:
The Idealist Legacy

Introduction

There are many today who are calling for a return to, or at least an increase in emphasis on school-based teacher education; and high among their reasons for advocating this is the belief that future teachers are getting too much theory in teacher education courses provided by the tertiary sector. It is commonly argued (and there is little new in this position) that the theory taught in initial teacher-education programs is unnecessary, or at best of low priority for future teachers: but it is now also being suggested that the theory component of pre-service initial teacher-education is actually harmful to beginning teachers in that it makes them too critical of the system they are being trained to serve.

I have strong reservations about these attacks on theory in general. But there is one small proviso. I too believe that the underlying basis of much of the educational theory taught in tertiary institutions today is harmful — not in the sense of developing teachers who are too critical, but rather harmful in impeding teachers' access to an adequate understanding of, and potentially worthwhile responses to, the provision of schooling and education in contemporary social conditions. That does not mean, however, that we must necessarily abandon theory and consign the whole of teacher-preparation to picking up functionary details in the classroom. Another response would be to modify the theory taught so that it better fits the reality of both classroom practice and the present political-economic situation and so that it better prepares teachers to respond to the educational challenges which confront them daily.

In the following sections I shall outline the central features of what I regard to be the dominant, but not the only, brand of educational theory underlying the offerings of today's tertiary institutions. I do this for three reasons. First, in order to understand the roles of schools and teachers in society it can be useful to recognize and comprehend the prevailing theoretic context, along with the historical and ideological position, in which such roles are placed, contextualized and defined. Secondly, outlining this theoretic context will also serve to highlight its deficiencies as well as the major problems it both confronts and creates when it comes up against harsh reality. And thirdly, there are aspects and details that I want to rescue from it and appropriate to my own ends when I develop my own positive case later.

The Context of Idealism

In 1918 D.H. Lawrence wrote that 'The elementary school-teacher is in a vile and false position ... caught between the upper and nether millstones of idealism and materialism'; and that the elementary school was the place where idealism and materialism met 'like millstones', and where 'teachers and scholars are ground between the two' (McDonald, 1961, pp. 589–90).

It was a delightful metaphor; and although he was referring loosely to the 'idealism' of Whitehall's spokespeople on education and the 'materialism' of the factories waiting for school leavers, Lawrence was, and remains, largely correct. Teachers are caught and ground between idealism and materialism, although not quite the forms that Lawrence identified; and school is an important place (although not the only place) where these millstones meet.

Idealism and materialism, from a philosophical point of view, denote two distinct frameworks of thought and thus two clearly distinct and identifiable approaches to educational issues and schooling practices. Idealism builds on essentialism and formalism, and speaks of eternal truths and timeless social, moral and personal values and ideas. Materialism, on the other hand, is non-foundationalist and anti-formalist. It regards knowledge, values, theories and practices, including those relating to education, as deriving from non-essential material contexts.

It is idealism which has provided the background and basic presuppositions for most past and contemporary educational practice and theory; and which, although having recently faced challenges from Neomarxism, and presently encountering challenge from sources as varied as economic rationalism and post-modernism, is currently legitimated as the dominant educational theory of the present historical period.

This is not to say, however, that idealism represents the best or most valid theoretical context available at the moment. A number of interconnecting social and historical factors can affect the legitimation and dominance of particular theories or 'bodies of ideas' at any particular time; and very often what counts as much, if not more, than intrinsic merit is the site of the production of the theory and the status of the producers within that site.

Around the middle of the nineteenth century the production of legitimate educational theory was generally entrusted to men (literally 'men') of letters such as Matthew Arnold, John Ruskin and Herbert Spencer, dons in schools of classics and philosophy, such as Henry Sidgwick and S.S. Laurie, and the occasional political reformist (for example, Kay Shuttleworth) or practising innovator within an elitist and selective system of schooling (for example, Thomas Arnold, F.W. Farrar, Cardinal Newman). In more recent times education faculties in universities and tertiary colleges tended to become recognized as a major site for the production of legitimated educational theory; and it is by and large the theory employed and generated by certain professional experts in those institutions which became well placed to attain and retain dominance.

The concentration of recognized 'expert' educational theorists in universities and specialized colleges is a relatively new, and not a universally praised, phenomenon. The academic capture of educational theory was partly brought about by, but more importantly coincided with, the location and placement of pre-service teacher education in academic institutions. Ever since this occurred teachers and intending teachers have continued to meet as legitimate educational theory that which has issued from professional academic experts in 'education'; and legitimate educational theory has become manifest as a highly selected body of theory which a particular group of highly selective people has considered worthy of preserving and passing on. The group of people in question, as with the nineteenth century men of letters, closely approximates those whom Aronowitz and Giroux call 'accommodating' and 'hegemonic' intellectuals, and even more neatly fits with Gramsci's 'traditional intellectuals': people whose social position as intellectuals 'derives ultimately from past and present class relations and conceals an attachment to various historical class formations' (Gramsci, 1976, p. 3). And the vast bulk of the theory — the staple diet of idealist theory which teachers consume in their training period, are confronted within guides to their work and in the advice and policy statements of their mentors, and which they attempt to implement and are accountable to in their practice — becomes, as we shall see, through its derivation as a legitimating factor of historical class relations, more of a burden than a means of sustenance for teachers working through the reality of their classroom experience.

The Characteristics of Idealist Educational Theory

With idealist educational theory now introduced it needs to be made more familiar. This section will indicate what characterizes this theory as 'idealist'; and why it is a millstone or a theoretic burden for teachers.

Basically, idealist educational theory denies, ignores, misconceptualizes, and renders unproblematic certain important factors about the real world of daily experience and practice. It fails to lay due emphasis on actual manifestations of material existence; particularly the effects of changing economic pressures and reforms on the practice and provision of schooling and education. Five major points can be noted in this regard.

First, this theory assumes, either explicitly or implicitly, an atomistic stance to social relations. It lays out a context which displays teachers as free, autonomous, individual agents and it describes teacher practice within the terms of such a context. An emphasis falls on what the independent, autonomous individual teacher can or might do for individual pupils, and then through dubious extrapolation, on the gains and transformations which are hoped for from the accumulative effect of large numbers of independent, autonomous individual teachers interacting with larger numbers of less independent and less autonomous but similarly individual pupils. The theory thus appeals to the aspirations and capabilities of teachers as individuals, and teachers are, of course, individuals in one sense. The sting in the tail, however, is that the theory is well placed to both attribute blame for failure to teachers as individuals, as well as to reify 'teaching' and then also blame teachers as a category for failure and shortcomings with the education system itself. But the main problem here is that the theory does not account adequately, if at all, for non-atomized social constraints which might stand between the teacher-as-individual along with the pupil-as-individual and the fulfilment of prescribed ideals. For instance, a central factor like the increasing need for, and the actual role of, schooling in the production of a progressively deskilled and proletarianized work force (Braverman, 1975), which teachers-as-individuals teaching pupils-as-individuals can do little to combat or oppose, is ignored or rendered unproblematic. Overall, there is no adequate accounting for structural constraints, macro- or microeconomic constraints, or even the micropolitical influences of gender, class, age, race and colour.

Secondly, idealist theory conflates concrete social institutions with abstract ideals. The most common example of this is the conflation of schooling with education. Now schooling does, of course, have some connection with 'education', but the nexus is tenuous and contingent and anything but an essentialist association. Schooling has much to do with things other than 'education', and the nexus consistently woven between the two falsely represents schooling to its agents (the teachers), its charges (the pupils), and to its providers and beneficiaries. Theory which declares that the main business of schooling is 'education', or simply blurs the distinction between the two, presents teachers with fine ideals, noble hopes, admirable aspirations, and large-scale failure when it comes to the realization of these things in practice (which is not to deny that many teachers contribute significantly in the education of some of their pupils). The nexus, in fact, mystifies the function of schooling within both social relations and economic contexts, and in doing so it not only creates tension and pressure on teachers; it actually sets them up as targets. It makes teachers, and teacher educators, easily visible victims by presenting them as the obvious impeding or malfunctioning forces if and when schooling doesn't satisfactorily educate. In fact it is now becoming almost traditional to blame teachers and schools for certain 'global' economic problems, to charge them with overcoming such problems (thus the commonly proclaimed hope or belief in an 'education led' recovery from recessionary times) and to blame them again if the problems are not overcome, even though it has not been established anywhere that raising the levels of a country's educational offerings and skill base consequently raises that country's productivity or GDP, thus leading to a better economic environment.

Thirdly, idealist theory admirably concentrates centrally on notions such as 'democracy', 'equality', and 'personal autonomy'; but it less than critically also suggests that the social formations in, to and for which the theory is meant to apply are actually democratic and egalitarian, and do seriously desire to promote universally the type of personal autonomy spoken of. Now teachers might believe in promoting democracy, equality and autonomy, and strive as hard as they can towards these ends; but if they are working within social relations which are undemocratic, based firmly on inequality, and threatened by too much personal autonomy, then these teachers are likely to continually encounter constraints between what they are striving for and what they are able to achieve. They are likely to experience conflict between the theory which guides their practice and the actual outcomes of their practice — conflict which, in the long run, is not adequately accounted for by the theory itself. Democracy, equality and autonomy are undoubtedly fine ideals and deserve promotion; but if they are to become more than ideals then the social conditions within which they can be promoted and realized have first to be constructed.

Fourthly, idealism exhorts moral and intellectual prescriptions which have a nice ring to them and read well as a projection of what things might be like in the best of all possible worlds. These same prescriptions, however, can emerge as empty rhetoric in particular social conditions and historical periods. For instance, idealist theory continues to recommend fostering human development in certain directions traditionally deemed valuable, while the economic conditions likely to dominate the coming decades could render these ideals inoperable and devalue fostering such development in all but a small minority of the population. It would be nice if teachers helped all pupils reach their highest possible degree of individual development, led pupils as deep as philosophy and as high as art, as Whitehead (1929, p. 1) put it, or even simply developed the spirit of fraternity among all, encouraged cooperation, and promoted equality and justice. Concerns and ideals such as these are a common basis of general teacher-endeavour. They are, however, very difficult concerns and ideals to fulfil not only specifically at a time when formal schooling, inclusive of tertiary levels, is entering a phase where it is more likely to engage in frustration and containment rather than liberation of human potential, but also generally in the context of non-cooperative, unfraternal, unequal, unjust wealthy industrial societies. Again, a prior condition for fulfilling such hopes and prescriptions is the construction of social conditions in which they can be fulfilled.

Finally, but not exhaustively, idealist theory makes continued and untenable reliance on an a-historic account of human nature and social development in attempting to justify its observations and conclusions. It commonly accounts for failure to achieve particular ends through recourse either to human nature (postulating that people are naturally lazy, greedy, evil etc.) and/or to naive a-historical accounts of 'the way things are' and how they got to be that way which tend to distort and misrepresent causal relations, which take existing conditions as 'given' rather than brought about, and most importantly which fail to recognize that 'existing conditions' are actively created, maintained and recreated in the present. A common result is that actual existing dynamic problems are confused with causal factors. In this way existing problems that might well be confronted and addressed can be identified, and dismissed, as a series of causes which have brought about a situation that we are now stuck with. An interesting example of this form of argumentation, combined with a retreat to human nature, is provided by R.S. Peters (1966) when he says:

> In all social movements, whether they be religious, political or cultural, there is always the problem of the majority who do not care . . . The explanation of this familiar phenomenon, as well as the inefficacy of advocacy, is not far to seek. The majority of men are geared to consumption and see the value of anything in terms of immediate pleasures or as related instrumentally to the satisfaction of their wants as consumers. (p. 145)

Herein lies all the consolation necessary for teachers seriously endeavouring to put idealist theory into practice but somehow just not getting the results. After all, what can you do in the face of human nature and the way things are?

The Legacy of Plato

Idealist theory has maintained its dominance in the field of education throughout the last five generations which, despite the occasional schism, rift or conflict, have been characterized largely by continuity rather than dramatic or revolutionary change. A prominent 'progressive education' movement has existed since at least the 1920s, but this has been continually opposed and viewed with suspicion from within the 'establishment' and has commonly (quite definitively in 1957) been denounced as a failure. Deweyan pragmatism has also been very influential, particularly in the USA; but overall, in Kuhnian terminology (Kuhn, 1962), we have experienced a period of 'normal education', in which a paradigm nurtured in Victorian times has continued to prevail. This paradigm, which may be referred to as liberal idealism, has roots which wind back to, and are firmly implanted in, the works of Plato.

The roots in Plato are manifestly obvious in the writings of those who held the first chairs and lectureships when the legitimation of educational theory moved to universities and specialized colleges, and at times the scholarly production which emerged tended towards adulation. For instance, the highly influential S.S. Laurie (1902) went as far as to say 'with confidence' of Nettleship's celebrated lectures on Plato's *Republic* that:

> . . . if a clever young graduate who has been teaching for a year or two without thinking much about the greater question of

education, will shut himself up for a week with Nettleship's essay he will come out into his school afterwards . . . convicted, converted, regenerate, sanctified. A new sun will be shining by day, and a new moon by night. As a teacher, he will live henceforth in the atmosphere breathed by the minor gods. (p. 69)

I have less lofty hopes and something of a different purpose in introducing Plato and the educational system which he spelt out in his *Republic* here. The Republic was an imaginary figment; but the ideas Plato recorded in the dialogue describing its workings have had a profound and long-lasting effect in educational theory and practice. In fact it would not be too much to say that the history of liberal educational theory (which, as previously indicated is 'idealist' educational theory) has been a long and virtually continuous assimilation of Platonic ideas to changing contemporary conditions. For reasons which I trust will become obvious and relevant later I want to spell out three of the themes underlying the Platonic idealist educational tradition. These themes, notwithstanding local amendments, can be identified without undue difficulty whether we look in at the agora in ancient Athens or on virtually any modern University Faculty of Education.

The first theme has to do with the cognitive, intellectual nature of education. In Plato's proposal for the desired education of the future guardians of the Republic instruction was to be initially offered to every citizen, male and female. Early instruction, however, was limited to physical and instrumental skills. Tests (which would probably now be called 'performance indicators') were then carried out, cut-off points were introduced, and as more and more of the population were eliminated at each testing point the content which continued to be studied became increasingly abstract and 'intellectual'. Towards the top something akin to intense cognitive engagement in areas considered by Plato to be essential and worthwhile to the production and development of the wise and fully rounded person was being offered to the few whom it was judged could benefit from the exercise. Real education, as distinct from socialization and vocational training, was identified as cognitive struggle with essential intellectually demanding worthwhile content. For Plato there was wrestling with mathematics and the liberal arts. In later times this was translated into studying the classics. In the nineteenth century Matthew Arnold rephrased it as coming to know 'the best that has been thought and said in the world', although the proposed content changed hardly in essence. In the 1960s R.S. Peters made enormous mileage by building the disinterested pursuit of worthwhile knowledge and developing one's cognitive perspective into the criteria for the concept of 'education' (as distinct from 'training' etc.), and then by detailing the cognitive content, or curriculum, of his identified 'education' in terms of a number of clearly specified 'worthwhile activities' (Peters, 1966, chapters 1, 2, and 5) which, not surprisingly, differed little from the liberal pursuits of earlier times. Even more recently Bloom (1987), not without considerable support, has declared real education to entail cognitive struggle with traditional essentialist content, and has blasted American universities for 'closing minds' and failing new generations by passing over the essential disciplines in favour of such corruptions as 'media studies' and 'women's studies'.

The second theme to note was that real (idealist liberal) education, as distinct from the instrumental training which was initially offered to everybody, was suited only for a naturally disposed intellectual elite, who could be identified by testing. Plato had no doubts that not everybody is equipped or cut out for cognitive struggle with intellectual content, and that only the few had the desire and ability to undertake the effort involved and to seek the particular rewards that were on offer. Similarly Matthew Arnold (1964) seemed to have no compunction in declaring that:

> The mass of mankind will never have any ardent zeal for seeing things as they are; very inadequate ideas will always satisfy them. On these inadequate ideas reposes, and must repose, the general practice of the world. (p. 24)

and that (Super, 1962, Vol 6):

> Knowledge and truth, in the full sense of the words, are not attainable by the great mass of the human race at all. (p. 72)

Almost a century later R.S. Peters noted that, despite a now well-established tradition of the sort of universal compulsory scheme Arnold hoped might eventually remedy this situation, deep cognitive exploration along with serious social concern had not caught on universally or even widely, but rather was still the province and predilection of a minority. When it came to 'sweat and struggle' versus seeking 'immediate delight' Peters (1966) claimed that:

> This type of probing is not pushed very far by the majority of men. Their way of life over and above those things which they

do because of their station and its duties, because of general social rules, and because of palpable considerations of their interest, is largely the outcome of habit, social pressure, sympathy and attraction towards what is immediately pleasurable. (p. 154)

which, as we saw, he put down to the 'fact' that:

The majority of men [do not care, and] are geared to consumption and see the value of anything in terms of immediate pleasures or as related instrumentally to the satisfaction of their wants as consumers. (*ibid*, p. 145)

The third of Plato's themes to be highlighted here was that educated people were to direct their learning and acquired wisdom into the just rule and guardianship of the State. Plato sought to replace rule by heredity, military violence or nepotism with rule by intellectual merit, with schooling playing a significant part in the fair and equitable determination of sociopolitical power and class location. The small number who best mastered the program (supposedly the most intellectually able) were thus to achieve additional contingent elite social status (albeit, for Plato, without financial reward) by being made rulers or members of the ruling class. In their hands lay not only power but also the knowledge, the ideals and the values that society was to live by — a notion echoed two-and-a-half millenia later by F.R. Leavis (1930) who declared that:

The minority capable not only of appreciating Dante, Shakespeare, Donne, Baudelaire, Hardy (to take major instances) but of recognising their latest successors constitute the consciousness of the race (or a branch of it) at a given time. For such capacity does not belong merely to an isolated aesthetic realm: it implies responsiveness to theory as well as to art, to science and philosophy in so far as these may affect the sense of the human situation and of the nature of life. Upon this minority depends our power of profiting by the finest human experience of the past; they keep alive the subtlest and most perishable parts of tradition. Upon them depend the implicit standards that order the finer living of an age, the sense that this is worth more than that, this rather than that is the direction in which to go . . . (pp. 4–5)

In summary; for Plato schooling was to offer equal opportunity to everybody, sort people out fairly on intellectual criteria, sift out the less able who were then to live contentedly in their justly apportioned place, and direct the most able and worthy to the prestigious decision-making positions in society.

It is something of a paradox that one particular aspect of this last theme encountered significant resistance at the very time when certain social, political and intellectual conditions might have seemed to have been favouring it. By the second half of the nineteenth century Plato's unashamedly elitist social and educational theory, along with his theory of human ability and intelligence (leaning heavily as it did in the direction of heredity), was under challenge. In addition to this, more recent history and changing material practices had generated theories of equality, egalitarianism, liberty, mobility, and the rights and individual worth of all humanity, which those such as Voltaire, Rousseau, von Humbolt and Mill had given voice to. At much the same time industrial capitalism had brought about great migrations to the industrial and commercial cities, as well as the need to school everybody. And finally universal schooling was actually in the process of becoming a reality. Here, then, lay the first real historical possibility to make not just schools and education, but also positions of power and privilege, available to all.

Yet this did not occur. Rather, as educational practice and theory wrestled with the problem of reconciling Platonic idealist elitism with liberal egalitarianism, the elitist side of Platonism prevailed, and it did so by actually appropriating the egalitarian push. It is important here to consider in a little detail how this happened and what implications this has had for contemporary schooling and teachers.

Hopes of offering real education and genuine opportunity to everyone through the provision and practice of schooling were very seriously held by many within the liberal tradition. But such hopes were overwhelmingly confronted with prevailing idealist notions of human nature and beliefs relating to inherently differing human abilities, as well as with the problem of finding and deploying the financial resources required for actually bringing such a thing about. It was asked whether the attempt, nobly conceived, to universalize and democratize schooling and education, and possibly raise the intellectual and cultural standards of all, might do little more than interfere with the prospects of those who were truly capable of benefiting in the first place, and consequently be detrimental to society as a whole. Fears were expressed that compulsion and universality would lead to lower standards and debased education. Such fears linger on. T.S. Eliot (1967) took time off from his poetry in 1948 to declare that:

> . . . in our headlong rush to educate everybody, we are lower-
> ing our standards, and more and more abandoning the study of
> those subjects by which the essentials of our culture — of that
> part of it which is transmissible by education — are transmitted;
> destroying our ancient edifices to make ready the ground upon
> which the barbarian nomads of the future will encamp in their
> mechanised caravans. (p. 108)

and R.S. Peters (1966) more or less repeated the sentiment a generation
later:

> The problem created by mass education, which has not been
> satisfactorily solved by either the American or the English
> educational systems, is that of providing adequate avenues for
> self-realization in a way that does not involve a depreciation in
> the quality of education available for those who are gifted enough
> to benefit from it. (p. 87)

The same thoughts are very commonly expressed today, especially
with regard to tertiary and higher education.

What happened, basically, was that the issue of providing universal liberating education, along with equal social opportunity, became
incorporated into the wider issue of providing a form of compulsory
schooling which was increasingly taking on multiple functions. On the
one hand there was the educative function of providing high level
intellectual fare for those who could benefit from it; while on the other
hand there was the instrumental function of socialization (keeping the
kids in order, and offering minimal instruction in literacy, numeracy
and morals). As Peters put it, ostensibly descriptively but with a barely
suppressed value judgment: 'though education is the essence of a school,
schools must also fulfil functions of a more instrumental nature' (*ibid*,
p. 167).

Platonic idealist elitism was thus reconciled with liberal egalitarianism; and liberal education discourse shifted back from the concern to
provide universal liberal education to a concern to introduce 'the best
that has been thought and said in the world' to those who could truly
benefit from such an introduction — now within a context of compulsory schooling which has to accommodate the entire youth population
and which has multiple social functions to perform. It became generally
and comfortably accepted that the real job of the school was to perform
its 'essential' educative function as far as possible and for as many as
possible, but at the same time to provide the best of instrumentality

(arguably social control) for those who could not or would not benefit fully from the educative aspect, while simultaneously serving public needs by meeting, as best it could, the requirements of the job market.

Thus, long after Plato, educational theory and practice remain dominated by the three themes identified above. First; educative activities still tend to be identified as those requiring cognitive struggle with particularly intellectually demanding content, they are associated with specific essentialist content, and they are given special status in schools. Secondly; educated people tend to be identified as those who best assimilate and master what schooling ultimately offers. And finally the educated, bearing particular cognitive content and certificates testifying to their mastery of that content, are classed and proclaimed as best equipped to perform prestigious, supposedly intellectually demanding jobs, to occupy certain privileged social positions, to be entitled to form opinions and have them respected; or purely and simply in a more modern sense, to rule — ostensibly by merit. Conversely (and still within the third theme), those who are not intellectually gifted and/or motivated towards struggling with the liberal curriculum, and who fail to benefit from assimilating and mastering the school's essential values and content, are to receive instrumental training, socialization and basic instruction, and become the modern artisans of the contemporary Republic — namely the working class in industrial capitalist society.

Interestingly, as educational theory and practice remained content to be dominated by these themes, the stage also became set whereby economic rationalism, when it finally made its entrance, could embrace and suffocate an obliging bedfellow rather than have to engage a defiant enemy.

Implications for Teachers

Idealist theory can be comfortable in times of relative social stability and economic expansion, and especially so for teachers in elite and privileged schools. It is partly teacher-centred and gives teachers a form of control of curricula and the purposes of schooling. It offers rewards for educating, and built-in excuses to teachers-as-individuals for failing to educate or improve the lot of children. But it does not have much to do with the harsh, polluted, real classroom climate in which most teachers live and work, which any of those teachers will tell you is not quite the atmosphere breathed by the minor gods. As such the theory can eventually become very disillusioning. It can turn teachers to baser yet more sustaining fare, and have them abandon hopes of tingeing activities with visions of greatness and settle instead for a modicum of quietness and order as they assume a lesser role of disciplinarian and child-minder. Teachers such as these, as well as those who retreat into idealist apologies, face having to carry as a burden the light that was meant to lead them, and being ground down by the very theory which was meant to guide and sustain them. Finally, there is not much that is interventionary about it all. Teachers, as they were for Plato, are cast as conservative agents (of low sociopolitical status) in an extremely conservative process. They can act either as Arnold's man (sic) of culture transmitting (with a highly variable success rate) an essentialist curriculum of pre-ordained worthwhile knowledge and high culture, or they can be childminders and socializers.

Fortunately, not all teachers accept such theory, or such roles, unproblematically.

Chapter 2

Reactions and Adaptations

Introduction

Although idealism, and its later philosophical counterparts like liberal rationalism, retained dominance and maintained a form of hegemonic control of educational discourse and practice, not everybody, of course, saw things from that particular viewpoint. It had long been claimed by critics that the liberal idealist tradition had, for instance, simply taken a supposed causal relationship between liberal education and class and social location for granted; and that it was possible, indeed likely, that the reverse of what was being proposed might actually apply. It was increasingly suggested that, rather than one's class and social location being determined by the level of one's success in schooling, it might be, just as much if not more so, that pre-existing class and social location might determine the level of one's success at school. The Platonic tradition, it was suggested, may have been aware of one aspect of the political functioning of schooling, in recognizing schooling's instrumentality in determining class location; but it had not adequately considered the political function of the overall curriculum of schooling which, rather than being universally liberating (or at least potentially so), might in fact serve to reinforce existing class and/or power relationships and structures.

In the 1960s numerous challenges were made to the idea that 'education was the essence of schooling', and the claim was commonly made that schooling really assisted centrally in reproducing the existing relations of production and consequently reproduced class relations and class distinctions. Schooling, it was argued, in transmitting 'high culture' or what some referred to as 'the best that has been thought and said in the world', was hardly 'educating'. Rather, it was really engaging in a form of intellectual imperialism which perpetuated elements of ruling class culture and oppression unconnected and irrelevant to the real existential needs of the majority of the population. The curriculum was thus seen as class interest serving (as well as serving interests based on gender, race and colour); and schooling was regarded as politically conservative and reactionary in that it functioned basically to reinforce existing social and class relations. Schools and teachers, many maintained, should focus on the real needs and interests of the working class and other oppressed groups. Some even suggested that schools and teachers might engage in the task of social reconstruction.

It was not, of course, quite as simple as that; and there were probably as many variations within the overall reaction as there were reactors themselves. But at the risk of oversimplification I want, at this point, to consider three central themes that developed.[1]

Schooling, Reproduction and the Correspondence Principle

Mounting concerns relating to inequalities in society, and to schooling's failure to ameliorate differences that children actually brought with them to school, as outlined in the Coleman Report (1966), in Jencks' massive study (1972) and numerous other places as well, led to a newly-sustained concentration on the actual form of schooling itself. This in turn suggested to a number of theorists, practitioners and researchers the possibility that the very experience of schooling was in fact experience of class relations, work relations and dominance-subordinance relations; and that while schooling retained its existing form it didn't matter all that much what content was taught. Early exponents of this form of thought included Jules Henry, Paul Goodman and Jonathan Kozol. Further development of this theme resulted in P.W. Jackson (1968) referring to the daily taken-for-granted processes of schooling (obeying bells, pupils seeking permission to leave the room, holding up one's hand if one wanted to say something etc.) as the hidden curriculum; a concept consequently elaborated by Ivan Illich (1971) and Everett Reimer (1971) who saw the very process of schooling to be so pernicious that they passionately called for society to be deschooled.

At much the same time, as a result of a major resurgence of interest in Marxism and in line with trends in other fields, Marxist critiques of schooling were developing. The French philosopher Louis Althusser (1984) introduced the educational world to the mechanics of the 're-production of the relations of production', and to the idea of 'ideological state apparatuses'; while in America political economists Sam Bowles and Herb Gintis published *Schooling in Capitalist America* (1976), which quickly became established as the major radical critique of both the liberal view of schooling and the deschooling theory, and which also placed the 'correspondence principle' firmly on the educational agenda.

From all of this there emerged a realization that schooling itself was an apparatus of the state which played a crucial and central part in stabilizing society by reproducing the relations of production. For Althusser the school was the major ideological state apparatus securing reproduction of the relations of production largely through forming people as ideological subjects. For Bowles and Gintis experience of the social relations within schooling corresponded to experiencing the different work relations that school leavers were to enter depending on their length and form of schooling, and in this way schooling fitted the pupil to more or less compliantly accept future work relations. Thus schooling, it was suggested, largely irrespective of the content of the set latent or overt curriculum, and in marked contrast to the theories and hopes of Plato or Dewey, reinforced social inequality and reproduced the existing class and power structures of society.

Early work by educational theorists taking up these new insights was overenthusiastic and crude; and possibly none more so than my own. Following Althusser uncritically, I wrote (1979):

> ... education is not merely useless, it is positively counter-productive in fighting and overcoming ideology. Education forms and reinforces the dominant ideological views in a society and the consciousness that accompanies them: it can never 'raise consciousness', or create the conditions or promote the 'critical awareness' whereby the dominant ideology of an era can be recognized for what it is, let alone be attacked. (p. 141)

and I also wrote, following Bowles and Gintis similarly uncritically:

> Clearly, then, the conduct and process of education in a capitalist society corresponds neatly with the conduct and process of the work-place; and so what is learnt via the process of education can be carried over directly by and in individuals as part of the ongoing perpetuation of the existing modes of production and social relations. In a capitalist society education simply produces a particular consciousness; one suited to the capitalist mode of production. (*ibid*, p. 144)

That was crude reproduction theory at its worst. But it was not just crude and uncritical: it was also politically naive, and absurdly defeatist.

Reproduction theory and correspondence theory, however, notwithstanding certain crudities, embarrassing errors and oversimplifications, had more than a mere historical importance and were not without intrinsic and abiding merit.[2] The major points in their favour were that they clearly recognized and accounted for the intrinsically conservative reproductive nature of schooling, and that they nicely identified the idealist rationalizations for, and class bias of, both schooling and its curriculum. If nothing else an era of naivety had been blown away, and it is unlikely now that schooling could ever again be seriously proclaimed as an a-political neutral site for dispensing knowledge and education.

Two of the major arguments against reproduction and correspondence theory were that they ignored and/or denied the reality of the contested nature of schooling (and society); and that in so far as they relied on forms of structuralism for their theoretic basis they emerged as depressingly defeatist. They appeared to leave no room for movement or resistance, and they seemed to present teachers with no alternative other than to act as puppets and servants of capital. Paul Willis's publication, *Learning to Labour* (1977), notwithstanding its own weaknesses, was soon to bring these criticisms into sharp relief. As he said of crude reproduction theory and structuralism, unknowingly lampooning words that had not as yet been published: 'Everything fits too neatly' (p. 175).

But there was a third issue which sparked most of the reaction to reproduction and correspondence theory — namely its reliance on certain aspects of the Marx-Engels/Althusser theory of ideology. These aspects, along with the criticisms raised, will be considered later. Here it might be worth pausing to reflect on what the radical reactions noted so far offered teachers in a positive sense.

The answer is very little, if anything. Identification of the operation of the hidden curriculum served to implicate teachers further, virtually through every move they made, in the conservation and reproductive aspect of schooling. Ideas of deschooling pointed both logically and practically to disbanding the teaching force as a professional body, given that teachers operating in a deschooled society would work largely in an individualistic, even a-social context. Acceptance of the reproduction thesis and the correspondence principle largely reduced teachers to a position of increasing conservatism in that they seemed incapable of doing anything other than reproducing existing relations of dominance and subordination. It offered little hope, and indicated few if any points of entry whereby resistance, let alone social reconstruction, could be practiced. Althusser himself saw very few teachers being able to do terribly much against a system of ideological and repressive state apparatuses. He asked 'the pardon of those teachers who, in dreadful conditions, attempt to turn the few weapons they can find in the history and learning they "teach" against the ideology, the system and the practices in which they are trapped'; and having declared them 'a kind of hero', he continued (1984):

> But they are rare and how many (the majority) do not even begin to suspect the 'work' the system (which is bigger than they are and crushes them) forces them to do, or worse, put all their heart and ingenuity into performing it with the most advanced awareness . . . So little do they suspect it that their own devotion contributes to the maintenance and nourishment of this ideological representation of the School . . . (p. 31)

Unfortunately, it was also to turn out that precious little hope would be found in the resistance theory later propounded by Willis (1977) in his reaction to crude reproductionism. Willis certainly highlighted the defeatist nature of much structuralist-based reproduction theory, but his alternative proposal, along with his empirical data, showed every bit as much that, for all of their resistance and for all that teachers might do, working class kids still got working class jobs. Or in other words, the relations of production were being just as neatly reproduced beneath the messy resistance that Willis saw as characterizing school and society.

The Curriculum as Intellectual Imperialism

The second major reaction, while not ignoring the form or nature of schooling itself, looked to the content of the traditional liberal education curriculum and saw not 'the best that has been thought and said in the world', but rather a mode of intellectual imperialism which ignored the real needs of oppressed groups and instead perpetuated ruling class culture, interests, concerns, and ultimately oppression itself. Some broached the issue gently and with humour, as in the case reported of the ghetto child of colour asked in school how many legs a grasshopper has — to which it is replied: 'Man, I wish I had your problems.' Others were more direct. They carefully scrutinized the liberal curriculum looking for bias and ideologically loaded content; and concluded that the knowledge legitimated in schools served ruling class interests and at the same time devalued knowledge produced by and relevant to subordinated oppressed minority groups, as well as oppressed *majority* groups such as women, people of colour, and the working class. The general conclusion from such studies was that the school curriculum, largely representing ruling class knowledge, helped to support, legitimate and sustain existing patterns of power. It was thus overall an instrument of oppression in that it both failed to provide mobility for the working class and other oppressed groups, while at the same time it stripped them of their dignity, it failed to listen to their voices, and it told them where they stood in the world — namely that they were dumb, deprived and inferior.

Having reached this type of conclusion some then argued that oppressed groups, including the working class, had to reject outright rather than try to assimilate what is taught in schools, since existing school curricula were really a central tool of white, male ruling class domination. Thus Neil Postman was later to go as far as to question (in Keddie, 1973) teaching print literacy on the grounds that, for many pupils, becoming print literate could be a first step along the path to being controlled by ruling oppressors. In the place of school (i.e. ruling class) knowledge, so this theme ran, there had to be a curriculum, tied in with a whole changed schooling experience, rooted in working class culture, propagating working class knowledge, and based on working class needs. Similar arguments were advanced to promote the cause of women, people of colour and minority ethnic groups, and to develop curricula which propagated their knowledge and which were based on their particular needs.

Others, however, were a little more tolerant towards the existing form and content of schooling, and argued basically that what the oppressed had to do was appropriate these to their own needs rather than reject them. For instance, the study of great literature or classical music, it was argued, ought not be totally forsaken on the grounds of cultural preferences for spy novels and reggae, or gender preferences for female composers and authors; football should not dominate a school's activities just because the local area might have had a long association with the game; and history, mathematics and science could be every bit as valuable to the cause of the workers and the oppressed as they were to the bourgeoisie. The theory and practice of Paulo Freire (Freire, 1972a and 1972b) regarding literacy as the first and essential act of liberation, now significantly supplemented by Colin Lankshear (1987), indicates both a positive development of the viewpoint expressed by Postman and a significant difference from the fears he raised.

This overall form of reaction seemed, at first blush, to be a fruitful and exciting prospect for teachers seeking to do more than conserve and reproduce the existing class and power relations in society. But the excitement did not last. In the cooler light of more considered reflection many began to argue that teachers, or at least the kind currently produced, were not generally well placed to understand working class or other forms of oppressed experience or culture. They did not necessarily know what is best for subordinated groups, and they were hardly, given their life experience and professional training, necessarily bearers of knowledge, values and programs of action superior to that borne by the oppressed. It became more and more commonly suggested that teachers themselves might have much to learn from their charges; and that the proper tactic might be to engage in cultural interaction and exchange in order to find common ground on which to begin work, rather than attempt to plant in alien soil or impose what the teacher thinks the kids really need. It was even seriously suggested that teachers were actually irrelevant. As Michel Foucault put it (1977), in a slightly broader context:

> The masses no longer need [the intellectual] to gain knowledge: they know perfectly well, without illusion; they know far better than he and they are certainly capable of expressing themselves. (p. 207)

This sort of reaction led to a different approach being taken to the educational needs of the oppressed, and in the early days to the educational needs of the working class in particular. Rather than subscribe to an ideological-domination thesis suggesting that the working class might not understand things properly, many academics and teachers turned their attention to seeking out what the real roots and dynamics of working class consciousness might be. In doing so they dug further and further into what they tended to identify as 'culture' or 'cultural forms' — commonly characterized as an organic set of practices, knowledge and consciousness that the working class has, develops and lives by independently of, and often in opposition to, that propagated by ruling class dissemination and legitimation processes. This theme, in a sense a development of the line taken by Richard Hoggart's successors at the Centre for Contemporary Cultural Studies at the University of Birmingham, swept through the UK and the USA in the 1970s. It rode the waves of the 'new sociology' and radical developments in philosophy of education; it led a number of academics to go out among the working class to see what their life is really like; and it resulted consequently in the generation of a large amount of variably valuable ethnographic work and data.

There was a nagging problem embedded in this, however, and many researchers and theorists found there was a sting in the tail of the theory they were holding or pursuing. They had used broadly Marxist methodology to expose cultural and intellectual imperialism, along with essentialism and bourgeois ideology, underlying not just existing curricula but also the theory which legitimated those curricula. They had thus come to regard as anathema anything which hinted of cultural or academic imperialism, or which might be seen as supporting a position whereby anybody, including themselves, could be taken as knowing what the working class doesn't know but needs to know. In paradoxical fashion the charge of intellectual imperialism, once conveniently reserved for bourgeois idealists, became extended to, and levelled at, those well meaning left-inclined academics and teachers who genuinely sought to further the interests of the working class. For instance, John Krige (1981) described my previously quoted *Education and Knowledge* as 'the intellectual baggage of the missionary zealot, fervently stepping out into the world with a view to saving it'; and added, in a manner which left no doubt as to which of out the workers' or the academics' consciousness he (himself an academic) regarded as being superior:

> [Missionaries] are in for a shock. For the odds are that the not-so-submissive or ideologically crippled workers in capitalist society will tell them to piss off and go preach their message elsewhere — to gullible members of academia, perhaps? (pp. 42–3)

Raymond Williams (1963), who had often warned that 'the making-over of the workers' cause into the intellectuals' cause [was] always likely to collapse' (p. 263), appeared here to be vindicated. The attack on cultural and intellectual imperialism turned out, and it appears unwittingly so, to be a classic instance of hoisting oneself with one's own petard. Those who looked for and found intellectual imperialism dared not replace it with fare of their own. Teachers may have discovered or been shown what not to teach, but the criteria which disqualified existing curricula content also seemed to disqualify anyone else, and particularly those capable of applying the criteria, from proposing alternative content themselves.

The same endpoint was also arrived at from another, closely related approach which bordered on the area of moral responsibility and became caught up with the level of justifiable interference that teachers might make in their pupils' lives. Teachers, nobody seriously doubted, were in the business of forming the consciousness of new generations. What was open to question was how deeply, if at all, they should be involved in determining the direction in which such consciousness should be formed; and much of the debate surrounding this issue became similarly hoisted on a petard of its own making. The more it talked of moral and critical teachers developing free, autonomous, critical citizens the less it seemed to allow teachers to be directive regarding the content and values to be taught. Carl Bereiter (1972) summed up the situation well when he noted that:

> the ethos that tells [teachers] what qualities the next generation should have also tells them that they have no right to manipulate other people or impose their goals upon them. (p. 26)

From Cultural Imperialism to Intercultural Articulation

The problem with the whole of this situation was that it left open the question not only of who might develop curricula and determine the purposes of schooling, but also what the purposes of the curriculum and schooling themselves might be. If imposing any sort of curriculum could be taken as imperialist, and if teachers of subordinated groups might have more to learn than to teach, at least in the first instance, then it would appear that teaching and schooling ought be non-interventive and non-directive, and perhaps instead should key into pupils' cultural forms. This is the direction in which the 'cultural theme' outlined above has tended to go, and in more recent times a number of sophisticated developments have emerged. One of the most rigorously articulated of these has been presented by Jim Walker in his book *Louts and Legends* (1988); and the case presented there has particular significance to this work for two specific reasons. First, in developing his argument for cultural articulation Walker also discusses the justifiable levels and areas of power and control that teachers, and governments, should have in relation to the determination of curricula content and educational aims. Secondly, the notion of 'choice among options' is central to Walker's stance; and as the matter of 'choice' will assume increasing importance as this work continues to examine teacher-control of curricula and educational aims, Walker's position in this regard might well be considered.

Walker's case is based on the premise that students should be treated as responsible and autonomous individuals; and he sees their development as such to be a 'fundamental educational principle' to be overridden only by ensuring that education serves the common good. 'A fundamental value for the individual', Walker claims, 'given the common good qualification, is to be able and be in a position to judge for him or herself' (*ibid*, p. 170); and therefore 'morally acceptable and practically effective schooling':

> must be directed towards enhancing the freedom and power of pupils to make personally fulfilling and socially beneficial choices about how to live their lives, and . . . if education is to contribute to social change it will be through taking this direction. (*ibid*, p. 156)

'Schools', Walker claims 'have neither the right nor the power to pursue social and political change by any other route' (*ibid*).

Walker allows that teachers might ply their knowledge and values to the end of improving the lot of their pupils, but he insists that a central part of this should consist not of planning, directing, imposing or telling but rather 'an exercise in experimental intercultural articulation'. He concludes that:

> Educators are not in a position to plan pupils' futures for them nor . . . should they if they could. What they can do is strive to equip young people to make the best of their opportunities and, through wise approaches to curriculum, teaching and personal relationships, broaden young people's knowledge and abilities in ways that expand their options. (*ibid*, p. 155)

Walker argues that, rather than base policy and practice on equality of outcome or opportunity, we would do better to apply the criterion:

> what, consistent with the common good, maximizes the opportunity for *these* people to determine their own destinies? What options can be made available to them given their background and, more importantly, given the problems they presently face, as they see them and in line of development from their currently understood options? (*ibid*, p. 170)

Not surprisingly, then, in his policy suggestions Walker puts consideration and adaptation to existing concrete conditions for choice above attempting to create better social conditions; and neither the structural barriers and constraints that he recognizes nor the general principles of equity and equality *per se* are given primacy. Instead, Walker concludes:

An overriding issue for educational philosophy and policy is the determination of equity of opportunity and outcome in actual, concrete conditions of choice . . . individuals may choose options lower as well as higher in the socioeconomic scale. These may or may not be best for them, but it is up to them, not educators or policy makers, to judge what is good for them. (*ibid*, pp. 169–70)

For Walker 'the search for common ground is the only way of pursuing equitably the welfare of different groups and individuals'(*ibid*, p. 157); and thus 'common ground', choice and the expansion of options are to provide the basis for schooling and teaching based on intercultural articulation. This position will be considered further at a later stage.

Finding a Suitable Other

If imposing any substantive curriculum could be taken as imperialist, or if teachers have no special rights or expertise to propose goals for their pupils or for society, then it could be taken as following that deliberate intervention towards social and political reconstruction is actually beyond the province of teachers. If this were the case then policy and curriculum might best be taken out of teachers' hands and instead be given to others. The question arising from this would be: in whose hands should policy and curriculum be placed?

The current waves of economic rationalism, technocratic rationalism and other branches of New Right policy discourse have answers to this question, and these shall be considered later. Before doing that, however, I want to examine a commonly proposed suggestion, namely that educational policy and curriculum should be given over to the hands of government, to be controlled and formulated on a national basis. Such an idea could reasonably be expected to be a central platform of fascism, crude socialism or forms of democratic federalism; but interestingly it is hardly confined to such contexts. In this section I want to consider the position proposed by John White (1988), not just because it advocates a National Curriculum, but because it does so from a liberalist stance, and from which it specifically seeks to disempower teachers by denying them a privileged voice in curriculum determination and the formulation of educational aims and policy.

White's argument for shifting the broad framework of the curriculum from professional (teacher) to political (government) control rests on the notion that questions relating to the aims and broad content of education are intimately connected with notions of the kind of society we want to live in. For White they are thus 'as much political questions as issues of taxation policy or defence'. These political questions, White insists, given that in a democracy every citizen should have an equal right to participate in the control or exercise of all areas of political power, are 'to be resolved by the citizenry as a whole' rather than a sectional group; and thus White concludes that:

> The problem with leaving curricula in the hands of the teaching profession is that it is, after all, only one section of the citizenry and there is no reason why its opinions should be privileged over other people's. (*ibid*, p. 220)

However, following Rawls, Nozick, and Dworkin, White also claims that it is not for governments to promote conceptions of the good, and that in fact they would be exceeding their powers if they 'steered pupils towards determinate pictures of the good life'.

A potential impasse looms here. If educational aims carry with them some picture of the good society, and if, on a liberal view, government is debarred from laying down aims which encapsulate a view of the good life, then who shall determine educational aims? White rejects all elitist proposals in this area, including the intellectual elitism favoured by the Platonic liberal tradition, on the grounds that elitism of any sort offends against liberalism in privileging a certain view of the good life over others. In doing so he thus rejects the idea that educational aims, along with curricula control, ought to be left to the teaching profession, there being, as previously quoted, 'no reason why its opinions should be privileged'. But White also sees neutralism as untenable, and he concludes by sounding a familiar theme; namely that a justifiable government policy should seek to promote the autonomy of all and not favour some at the expense of others.

A 'justifiable government policy', for White, includes the formulation of a National Curriculum. He adds, however, that such a curriculum can be defensible only if it is genuinely committed to democratic principles, including equality of political power; that it must include 'among its goals preparing all young people to become equal citizens of a democracy' (*ibid*, p. 220); and that liberal democratic governments should have 'extensive responsibility . . . for laying down educational aims which prepare their citizens for autonomy' (*ibid*, p. 229). The curriculum, for White, must be designed to acquaint pupils impartially with a whole range of different ideals of the good life, without steering them towards any ideals in particular; and he concludes that, while there is, in theory, a strong case for government control of the curriculum:

> There are no grounds for allowing any *section* of the population to determine aims, since any serious account of the latter will bring with it some picture of how society is to be, and since this picture is no private and fleeting vision, but is intended to inform the workings of public institutions, *every* citizen, and not only a sectional group, has an interest in the subject. There is thus no reason why teachers should have any privileged voice; or parents; or teachers and parents together. (*ibid*)

Aims, for White, are to be publicly determined, by governments favouring aims related to their role. Thus 'in a liberal-democratic society the proper task of government is to promote the well-being of all citizens by equipping them with the necessary conditions of an autonomous life' (*ibid*). White recognizes that it does not follow from his argument that it is necessarily wisest for a liberal democracy to put the aims of education under government control, but what does follow is less than conclusive. White leaves us with a hazy picture of government representatives working with professional educators, under the possible protection of a constitutionally enshrined code of educational principles premised on the promotion of autonomy for all.

Interestingly, the faltering and lack of clarity here, which is characteristic of liberalism, in this case leaves the particular argument (as well as liberalism itself) wide open to appropriation by the current rhetoric of devolution and choice. And yet, paradoxically, there does not appear to be too much in it, on White's account, for the commonly proposed beneficiaries of devolution and choice, namely teachers and parents. There also does not seem to be much respect for them either. Instead, a mysterious other — mysterious since, as I have shown elsewhere (Harris, 1990), White is confused regarding the identities of the 'citizenry', the 'community' and the 'government' — is granted easy privilege with regard to formulating educational policy and determining school curricula.

Conclusion

There are a number of significant similarities in the reactions noted above. All agree with Platonic idealism that a major goal of education in liberal democracies is the development of autonomy, although they might see the development and the nature of autonomy differently. All also agree, against Platonic idealism and despite apparent differences regarding the extent to which government policy makers might determine curricula, that government should not impose notions of what is good for people. All advocate diversity and pluralism, and all are opposed to teachers adopting monistic viewpoints. All advocate the value of choice and insist that individuals must be allowed to choose freely and execute personal commitments and projects, rather than have these imposed on them by others. Walker goes further than the rest to suggest that, given certain broad qualifications, it is best that people themselves judge what is best for themselves.

I shall consider the matter of 'choice' in some detail later. At this point I shall simply note that the major provisos put forward with regard to freedom of choice are White's insistence that people do not infringe certain democratic principles, which he fails to specify adequately; and Walker's qualification that free and autonomous choice be subject to a 'consistency with the common good' clause, within which the key notion of the 'common good' (along with how it is to be determined) is similarly left vague and unspecific. It is more important to recognize, however, that in their own ways all of the reactions noted above oppose teacher determination of the content and purposes of schooling. All are concerned about, and oppose, albeit for different reasons and in different ways, teachers having a privileged voice regarding curricula and notions of the good.

Notes

1 To do justice to all involved would require reviewing an immense production of literature spanning two decades: to presume to highlight 'leaders' of each theme would be to engage in dangerous value judgments and to ignore the fact that many researchers modified their views in the course of time and experience. Central and commonly identifiable contributors to the literature, along with others referred to in the text, include Louis Althusser, Jean Anyon, Michael Apple, Basil Bernstein, Pierre Bourdieu, Samuel Bowles, Martin Carnoy, Paulo Freire, Herbert Gintis, Henry Giroux, Paul Goodman, Ivan Illich, Richard Johnson, Nell Keddie, Herbert Kohl, Jonathan Kozol, Henry Levin, Rachel Sharp, Geoff Whitty, Paul Willis and Michael F.D. Young.
2 Fortunately, after a period of negative over-reaction useful defences, for example, Gumbert (1988), Cole (1987), are now appearing.

Chapter 3

Teachers, Materialism and the Real World

Introduction

The previous chapters may have given the impression that educational policy, schooling practices and the job of teaching are driven, directed and determined by theoretic concerns and debates. This is hardly the case. Practice and policy are, of course, theory related and theory implicated, but theory, notwithstanding idealist hopes and fantasies, does not dictate to the real world. It is more the case that the production of educational theory, along with establishing related practices such as the formulation and implementation of curricula, striving towards educational ends and outcomes, and fostering specific skills etc., are determined by existential material conditions relating to social practices, issues and problems, and are influenced strongly by the level of control and power that identifiable interest groups have over circumstances at any particular time.

This, at least, is the broad materialist position, and the one that will be followed in the rest of this book.

Materialism recognizes human beings to be sociohistoric manifestations of biological reproduction rather than pure emanations of human nature, and it sees educational values, theories and practices as deriving not from some essential basis but rather from historical material contexts. In materialist terms education has no essential form or timeless universal nature. Rather it is to be understood and determined by analyzing particular material contexts, and the interests and needs involved therein. In a particular form of materialism which I will incorporate to some extent later, economic determinants are regarded as the central and basic conditions influencing practice.

The distinctive nature of the materialist approach can be seen in its account of the operation of universal compulsory schooling, which is a useful place to begin, a second time, to consider the past and especially the future role of teaching.

Universal Compulsory Schooling and Production Relations

In the early nineteenth century the Western world experienced the establishment of radically altered socialized and collectivized production processes, and along with this massive migration which concentrated large populations in industrial and commercial cities. As this occurred the traditional family unit became increasingly expelled from the production process; and consequently its informal educational function became delegitimized. A three-fold need thus arose. Reproduction of labour power had to be rationalized, in the sense of inculcating attitudes and values in future workers which, rather than being specific to performing particular jobs, were conducive to accepting and promoting certain general newly-developed social and production relations. An institutionalized transition from family relations to collectivized work relations was also needed. And an alternative arena became necessary for passing on the actual skills and knowledge required by the newly collectivized workers — skills and knowledge which the family alone could no longer provide. A single answer to all these needs was the establishment, by the state, of 'free', compulsory, universal elementary (and later secondary) schooling.

Almost two centuries later, and notwithstanding developments in educational practice and theories, universal compulsory schooling continues to function largely as it did in the beginning, as the intermediary institution between the family and the labour market (a point not unnoticed by economic rationalism). As such it does three basic things.

First, schooling provides certain skills and knowledge required by most, if not all, future workers (for example, literacy, numeracy), as well as socially-specific highly valued esoteric skills and knowledge for a small proportion of pupils headed for specialized regions in the labour market. Secondly, it transmits to all future adults, albeit with varying degrees of proficiency and success, the values, norms and attitudes required by people occupying different positions within the existing relations of production. And thirdly, it diverts part of the cost of producing trained and pre-sorted workers for the labour market from the employers to the state, or more specifically to the taxpayers. If there has been any serious major change in recent times it has been that developments in macro- and micro-economic policies have tended to promote moves to divert a larger share of the cost (and the effort) of producing employees away from employers and more directly to the taxpayer and the taxpayers' progeny who are now represented as *consumers* as well as beneficiaries of schooling.

The last of those points is especially important, indicating as it does that, along with the transmission of knowledge, skills and values, schooling also serves an important role within the economic structure or dimension of the state. Examining the operation of schooling within such a context is in turn especially useful. It can reveal generally the function schooling serves within social relations, and it can indicate specific matters such as why, in the present context, particular changes relating to the 'marketization' of schooling and the deprofessionalizing of teachers are taking place so widely and commonly.

Idealist liberal theory, it will be recalled, in attempting a reconciliation with egalitarian programs, became committed to the principles that all should be educated, in the sense of achieving 'the highest degree of individual development of which they are capable' (Nunn, 1921, p. 12), or having their powers extended and developed to the full; and it declared the central function of schooling to be getting on with that educating. It did not, however, despite the carefully wrought nexus between schooling and education, see contemporary schooling as being exclusively concerned with such 'educating'; nor did it expect all pupils to emerge from the schooling experience as nicely or equally educated people. Constraints on schooling and on individual pupils were commonly recognized. But what this theoretic context totally failed to recognize or acknowledge is the economic impossibility of, in its own terms, 'educating' everybody under existing social conditions; and the related economic impossibility (and political naivety) of having the liberal education and personal development it speaks of as the main business of the school. This, while it is to a large extent related to how much money the Treasury has, and what proportion of Gross Domestic Product the government might desire or be able to lay out on schooling, can be better understood in terms of production relations. I will now examine the relationship of schooling to production relations; first in the context of Marx's classical identification of 'productive labour' and 'unproductive labour' and the interrelation of these in political economy (Marx, 1961 and 1969), and then in the contemporary context of the adoption of corporate managerialism as part of a process of effecting the transition of the welfare state to the competitive state.

Production Relations According to Marx

Marx's categorization of productive and unproductive labour provides a highly valuable analytic tool, and one that can be largely utilized without further recourse to many elements of the overall Marxist research program. The distinction between the two forms of labour is made in terms of exchange relations. Productive labour is labour exchanged with capital to produce surplus value or profit (for example, labour expended assembling TV sets at Matsushita Electric Co.). It is thus the very source of capital accumulation, which in turn is the basic requirement for maintaining the capitalist mode of production, and its attendant social relations. Unproductive labour, on the other hand (for example, working in the public service, teaching in a government school, providing personal service to an entrepreneur), is not exchanged with capital, and does not produce surplus value directly. It is usually exchanged with revenue, as in the case when government employees are paid for performing public and welfare services; and revenue in turn is largely (but not only) made up from part of the surplus produced by productive labourers, and is most commonly (but not only) manifested in taxes.

A key issue can now be recognized. Since virtually the entire expenditure on state-provided and state-assisted schooling (including higher education) presently comes from taxes, or largely from a part of the surplus generated by productive labour, schooling is basically a drain on surplus and thus a potential threat and impediment to capital accumulation.[1] And this threat has been further compounded by historical developments within capitalism which have resulted in a dramatic increase in the proportion of unproductive labourers in the workforce. The small proportion of such labourers participating in the workforce when universal compulsory schooling began has grown to a present day level of around 40–50 per cent. This means that, if present production relations are maintained, about half of the population now passing through schools who later get jobs will engage in unproductive labour; and they, along with those who do not enter the labour market, will not directly generate surplus value. Given that this could account for upwards of 70 per cent of the children compelled to attend school for at least ten years, it is clear that contemporary schooling has become more than an inefficient contributor or a potential threat to capital accumulation. It has in fact become an extremely serious drain on surplus value: sufficiently so to generate unprecedented political concern regarding its financing and restructuring in advanced capitalist societies.

The drain on capital brought about by schooling must be offset or plugged up if accumulation is to continue. This could be done either through modifying the provision and financing of schooling, through increasing the productivity of existing productive labourers, through restructuring production relations so that some among the present unproductive force become productive contributors to surplus, or by any combination of the above. One obvious potential solution would be to modify the 'universal' and/or 'compulsory' aspects of schooling. State schooling might be made non-universal by offering it to fewer people, perhaps selectively through testing; or less universal by encouraging a drift or defection to privately provided schools. It could be made non-compulsory, or less compulsory, through lowering the minimum leaving age or by reverting to a past practice of making attendance at each higher level subject to examination success. But none of these things, all of which have been vigorously mooted in contemporary debates, could be achieved with sufficient comfort in the present conjuncture (apart from the very obvious failure in many countries to discourage a drift to private schools). On the one hand, existing ideological commitment to universal compulsory schooling is extremely strong; which is partly testimony to both the traditional underpinning pervasiveness of idealist liberal theory and the perceived effectiveness of schooling in reproducing existing relations of production. And on the other hand there are political, as well as conflicting economic needs to actually extend rather than merely maintain the present form and length of schooling. These needs, which relate generally to having schooling better serve the labour market through doing more towards the production of productive labourers, have driven various proposals, outlined in a plethora of recent reports, from raising the school leaving age,[2] through restructuring the provision of tertiary and higher education to better fit the needs of industry and the labour market in general, to making school curricula more relevant to employment skills.

Under the last two of these proposals expenditure on schooling could directly counteract the drain on capital accumulation simply by enhancing the basic training of future productive workers at school. If this were done productive labour would require less training elsewhere (such as in technical, further or higher education — or on the job); and future productivity might even offset not just the drain but also the increased cost of reproduction, given that schooling is getting dearer to provide. But again so simple and obvious a solution turns out to be less simple and less easy to effect than it might at first seem.

Two things stand in its way. First, what would suffer considerably would be the 'liberal' and 'educative' function of schooling. The result would be a marked divorce between a historically established and continuing rationale for the role of schools in fostering education and promoting something like 'the highest degree of individual development' of each child; and actual practice which would elevate and promote the instrumental function of schooling as the norm. Until quite recently the case to retain the 'liberal educative' model of schooling would easily have held sway. Now, however, a fierce ideological battle is under way to delegitimate that 'traditional' view by indicating that, for all its intrinsic merit, it is out of tune with contemporary conditions; and within the context and intellectual discourse of economic rationalism the move is very seriously on to elevate the instrumental aspect of schooling.

Secondly, since the specific problem facing capital is not that of merely reducing a drain, but of reducing a drain brought about largely through schooling so many who will not be future productive labourers, such a restructuring could only succeed if a large majority of school pupils were headed in the direction of productive labour. That may have more closely approximated the situation when universal compulsory schooling was first instituted, but, as indicated above, this is no longer the case. And the growth in the numbers of future potential unproductive labourers raises a closely related complication. Labour relations have become historically constructed in such a way that it is the unproductive labourers who tend to stay on longest at school, engage more with the traditionally recognized cognitive intellectual pursuits, and whose production is regarded and displayed as the paradigm instance of the school performing an educative function for society. To fail to concentrate on this function, and/or to crudely redirect school resources to increase productivity by decreasing the number of unproductive labourers, would again focus an unwelcome emphasis on the instrumental function of schooling; and in this area the purveyors of economic rationalism have once again appropriated and fostered aspects of liberal idealism in their ideological struggle to make that emphasis positively welcome.

Everything, however, does not hang on achieving a successful 'internal' modification of schooling directed towards producing fewer unproductive workers. Much the same economic outcome can be achieved 'externally'. Trivial (if tangible) results can be achieved by any of the increasingly proliferating schemes presently under consideration or use, which employ variations on the 'user pays' principle. Having students pay for their own schooling, either through voucher systems, loans, fees, or a tax on their future salaries, clearly requires less input from, and thus less drain on, capital. But there are dangers

and counter-productive tendencies in such schemes. A much more significant and global effect can be achieved by modifying production
relations themselves in order to redirect present unproductive labour
into the realm of the productive.

Such modification has been taking place gradually within corporate capitalism over the last two decades, through varied means such as
winding down the public sector, using technology to phase out service
jobs such as typing, inter-office deliveries, making coffee etc., and
eliminating strata of middle management through employing line-
management forms of administrative processes. It has, however, sud-
denly gained pace dramatically in places such as the UK, Australia and
New Zealand through a practice once considered unthinkable by many,
namely privatization. Under this scheme the state sells certain institutions and functions, such as the railways, the telephone and postal
systems etc., to private enterprise under the banners of 'choice', 'efficiency', 'participation', 'sharing the wealth' and 'handing public institutions back to the public', and whatever else might be achieved in the
process, this move also changes the status of the labour involved. Labour paid for by the state, necessarily out of revenue, is unproductive;
and privatization immediately ensures that most of the same labour will
now have to generate surplus if it is to be retained, and that it will be
paid for out of surplus, thus becoming productive. This, it must be
stressed, is not just a matter of definition. On the one hand the labour
will only continue in the form of a paid job if it secures capital accumulation, creates surplus and is thus deemed worthy of being funded.
In this context a number of jobs that governments once put to the
service of the public could simply be eliminated as the private sector
seeks to achieve precisely what is expected of it — making a profit —
by doing the very thing the state could not do or at the least would not
be generally popular for doing, namely trimming the labour force. And
on the other hand the state, through handing over sources of profit to
capital, thus further helps to secure capital accumulation. This in turn
leaves the state with less money of its own to manage, and so provides
a form of fiscal 'justification' for the state to offer less services (usually
less welfare services) within a proclaimed context of 'rolling back
control', promoting devolution and seeking minimal intervention in a
free market economy and a 'free market' form of social relations.

The state, however, can not totally privatize its own civil or public
service, although this too is actually being mooted; and there have
even been calls for the complete privatization of schooling. The most
the state can do in this regard is cut back its services and administration. It cannot totally relieve itself of unproductive labour, but it can, in

with the process of minimizing services, change the entire microeconomic interrelationships among unproductive labourers to significant ends.

Production Relations According to Corporate Managerialism

Another major accommodation that the state has taken in response to downturns in growth and economic recession (that is, reduced capital accumulation) is to adjust its administrative structural processes in the direction of corporate managerialism. This move, prompted by the need to internationalize capitalist ventures in response to what is in fact a global recession, basically involves reshaping the microeconomy relating to the administrative structures of the public sector, so that that sector no longer services a welfare state but rather a state seeking a competitive market edge in a transnational economic context. The fact that states are conceptualizing their placement transnationally can be seen in major overt actions such as present moves to establish a unified European Economic Community and in the repositioning of the USA and Australia with regard to Asian-Pacific markets, as well as in little things like the Prime Minister of Australia bowdlerizing a famous poem to declare 'the vision splendid' of the 1990s to be 'to internationalize Australia'.[3] The discourse of economic rationalism then seeks and promotes ideological legitimation of this move by translating what were once spoken of as public or social goods into commodities allegedly best considered in the economic arena of the market place.

In this context the state changes its orientation and priorities, and shifts its resources away from internal welfare provisions and towards positioning itself favourably in the milieu of international economic competition. As this occurs public and welfare services are scaled down where possible, and as less funding in real terms goes into them central government administration becomes less able (and less concerned) to secure and maintain former levels of quality control. This in turn encourages the financially privileged to opt out of the public system and turn instead to the private sector for what had historically become public services (for example, health care, education). As these services are then progressively turned over to the market productive rather than unproductive labour (as in the context of the previous section) is thus increasingly employed. Also, insofar as these services continue to exist as public services, the orientation changes from the delivery of services or goods to the skilful management of commodities and fixed resources.

Recent developments relating to restructuring the administration of schooling in New Zealand, Australia and the UK, for instance, show the state not just clearly and deliberately regearing the structure of schooling (at all levels) to the changed needs of capital, but also changing the accompanying rhetoric such that schooling and education become referred to, and naturalized, as commodities rather than public goods (Grace, 1988). In an incredibly short period of time the word 'administration' has been despatched down a form of Orwellian 'memory hole' to be replaced by 'management'. In educational institutions administrators and principals tend now to be referred to as 'senior management' while classroom teachers are also beginning to be referred to and regarded as managers of resources — this latter term having been stretched to now include both knowledge and pupils. In addition to this, management, along with a large degree of accountability for quality control, has been devolved to the local level, such that with regard to education it is the local school rather than the government which is now becoming increasingly accountable to the community.

But the change has not been merely linguistic. Practices too have changed. Schools and teachers are being required to be more efficient in cost-benefit terms, which is not bad in itself but which becomes suspect when cost is rendered finite and absolute through block grants or bulk funding within which teachers have to educate as best they might while also balancing a tight budget, and where efficiency is tending to be measured on narrow easily quantified performance indicators such as pupils' results in standard attainment tests, or utilitarian functionary indicators devised to measure teaching competency. Organizational principles of line management transferred from business corporations to schools are tending to destroy the collegial atmosphere of school and educational decision making, and to serve to deprofessionalize teachers in the process. Teachers along the line spend valuable time checking and monitoring the output of others in the line (who are currently well educated professionals), as well as suffering the need to engage in increasing paper shuffling. Growing practices like appointing managers from outside of schooling instead of principals who have come up through the teaching service and who understand the needs of teachers and pupils is similarly destroying the collegial atmosphere as well as damaging teachers' potential career paths. Individual contracting and the introduction of fixed term contracts for teachers has created competition among teachers both throughout the service and within particular schools, once again seriously affecting the collegiality that has for so long beneficially marked school relations. Attacks on unionism itself, and the increasing use of practices which render unions marginal, such as individual contracting and local hiring of school staff, have left teachers with less defensive support and has made them both more vulnerable and more likely to resort to self-regarding individualistic and competitive strategies. Teachers' duties have been extended far beyond the educational realm, as they are literally forced to take on managerial trivia such as calculating and levying electricity charges to accompany hiring of the school hall, or find themselves responsible for collating points in fund-raising schemes initiated by businesses (commonly computer companies, supermarket chains and fast-food franchises) outside of the school. And schools themselves have been put in competition, often totally unfair competition, with each other as they exercise new freedoms to tout both for pupils and for sponsorship dollars, and as they 'market' (the word *has* become a verb) their offerings and commercialise what was once primarily a potential educational exchange. The Coca Cola High School, the McDonald's Gymnasium and the Kentucky Fried Chicken Softball Team are no longer figments of a cynical imagination.[4] As resources for schooling begin to be doled out in bulk grants it is not too surprising to find schools, and teachers, paying lip service to educational ideals and practices and concentrating instead, and necessarily so, on balancing a budget and seeking success within the competitive ethos of the schooling market place whilst attempting as best they can to live within their means. As indicated earlier, the areas over which teachers are required to exercise management skills are increasing while the areas over which they can exercise professional expertise and judgment, such as policy debate and curriculum, are dramatically decreasing.

What has been said above is not, of course, exactly the way in which the changes towards corporate managerialism have been publicly articulated. Rather, the public has been told, through carefully orchestrated statements and reports issuing from government departments and less formalised government-created 'think tanks' such as England's 'Social Affairs Unit' and New Zealand's 'Education Forum', that existing education systems were financially wasteful, that they were too centralized, that they were failing to bring about social mobility, that they had become unresponsive to and out of touch with modern times, and that basically what was needed was a complete rethinking of the entire issue of the provision of schooling. The push behind corporate managerialism and economic rationalism was then based on offering people local control, choice, active democratic participation, and the virtues of the market-place as a necessary and viable alternative to an outdated overgrown centralized bureaucracy which was already the subject of widespread dissatisfaction and whose perceived deficiencies were then dramatically displayed and laid out for the people. The ideological nature of this move will be considered later.

A New Role For Schooling and Teachers

What corporate managerialism means for teachers in their day-to-day work recontextualized as management of schools, pupils and the distribution of knowledge, has been sketched out above. The question that might now be considered is how the once gradual and now rapidly accelerating redirection of labour from the unproductive to the productive realm, within the context of the move to corporate managerialism, can be expected to impinge on the broader role of schools and teachers.

The first thing to recognize is that capital must continue to accumulate if any social formation is to survive, and thus the primary role of any state is seeking to secure conditions conducive to capital accumulation. That task might be described as 'fostering economic growth' or even as providing security for all workers and citizens, but it all washes up the same in the end. Without capital accumulation any society collapses, in the way so much of Eastern Europe has recently collapsed — that is, with economic collapse preceding and determining political and ideological collapse; and it is the function of the state to act as a relatively autonomous power-structure seeking to secure conditions conducive to the accumulation of capital so that such political and ideological collapse does not occur.

How the state undertakes that task is a historically contingent matter. It may attempt to produce more cheaply and efficiently, apply human capital theory to education, change the nature of production relations, seek to become more competitive internationally and so on. But if capital accumulation is to continue with minimal political disruption and minimal educational and ideological disjunction in the present historical moment we could expect to see an interactive application of all the developments noted in the previous sections. Schooling's growing expenditure on both productive and unproductive labour is most likely to be offset by seeking to increase the return from expenditure on present productive labour, as well as by making present unproductive labour more productive in the future (O'Connor, 1973; Harris, 1982). We are also likely to see continued devolution and line management, along with what stems from that.

The effects of these moves are already evident in schools, in government proposals and reports (so many of which see new forms of management and new structures as the key to improving education) and in newly implemented policies. Concentration in schools has been directed, and almost daily becomes increasingly directed, to formal disciplined transmission of the 'basics'; i.e. those skills required by all future workers, while ideological rationalizations repeat the perennial claims that standards are falling and that child-centred teaching methods are largely to blame. In this context ostensibly supportive reports such as Alexander, Woodhead and Rose's *Curriculum Organisation and Classroom Practice in Primary Schools* (Alexander *et al*, 1992; commonly referred to in the UK as the 'Three Wise Men Report') tend to be eagerly and readily accepted by representatives of the state. And the open emphasis, hammered in report after report, on the role of schooling in job orientation and preparation is also growing daily; commonly rationalized by the dubious claim that having pupils learn marketable skills in school will make a significant contribution to overcoming unemployment. Schools, and with them universities and other sections of higher education, are being asked, and forced, to concentrate on discipline, to put aside child-centred methods and self-directed learning techniques, to 'cut out the frills' and to be more efficient, which tends to mean reducing both the breadth of options offered and the number of liberal options offered, and instead to direct effort towards making pupils employable, more so now at the productive level. Finally, state funding has been massively redirected away from the public service sector, as a result of which schooling and higher education, notwithstanding bulk funding, have suffered substantially, resulting in larger classes, fewer resources, less options etc., which has placed greater strain on teachers and which has made them even more vulnerable and open to blame should the mythical education-led recovery not materialize. Simultaneously, within the public sector itself funding has been directed away from liberal arts programs towards specifically selected vocational and technical programs. Thus at one and the same time valued abilities are being redefined, and the entire schooling system is being asked to produce greater numbers of modified desired end-products, all with less direct input from capital. The eventual graduates, irrespective of whether the numbers at the higher end will increase or not, are likely to have neither the form nor the level of cognitive development that idealist theory traditionally advocates. Idealist theory might still linger in academia and other enclaves of traditional intellectuals, and still infiltrate educational policy statements in a rationalized way, but now, as global recession seriously threatens both the pace and even the possibility of continued capital accumulation, it finds itself more at odds with economic reality than it has ever been. This has particular consequences for schooling, education and teachers in the contemporary situation.

In order to recognize these consequences we can begin with a point of basic economics which has been touched on before; namely that globally, if capital accumulation is to continue, the cost to society of unproductive labour must at least be counterbalanced by the production, at minimal cost, of productive labourers equipped for increased productivity. Therefore the success schooling has regarding turning children into unproductive labourers (which, regardless of privatization in some areas, it will continue to assist with) must be at least balanced by the production of more productive workers. The production of the former impels the production of the latter. Now unproductive labourers generally, although not universally, do more schooling and in higher streams, undertake more 'intellectual' studies, attend beyond the point of legal compulsion, and need higher certificates in order to first obtain their particular jobs. Also, the type and content of schooling encountered by future unproductive labourers, at least in the later years, still coheres, even if decreasingly so, with idealist liberal educational theory which has always been more in harmony with the particular production, as in the past, of a small highly-schooled, supposedly intellectually superior social elite. It thus turns out that children elevated or directed into unproductive levels, or 'educated' in the cognitive-intellectual sense (and they are not necessarily the most able children) are so elevated, developed, directed, or 'educated' at the expense of others who must, at the basic bedrock level of economics, see the ideals of liberalism evaporate before them. The end result, if only some can have what many are capable of benefiting from, is massive and increasing global wastage of human resources and potential.

The situation, then, is that after a period in which more 'education' has been offered to more and more people, we have reached a point where it has been deemed necessary and appropriate to both change the skill base of unproductive labourers and to produce more productive labourers equipped for increased productivity. The present situation is that while idealist notions still linger and are championed by some traditional intellectuals who have been well served by them, and while schools and teachers will continue to assist in the education of unproductive labourers, the number and proportion of these labourers are highly likely to decrease, and their required skill level and intellectual development (as classically defined) will certainly decrease. As privatization gathers pace it is likely that entrepreneurs will continue the existing trend of taking on, directly or indirectly, the narrow, specialized instruction of their most-skilled functionaries, and leave schools with the task of socialization and basic training of the largest body of newly-defined productive labour. And even if there is to be an increased number of university graduates, as so many governments' proposals for restructuring higher education want to insist there will be, then, as indicated above, these people are unlikely to possess either the type or level of intellectual development and excellence traditionally promoted by idealist theory. That particular educational currency is being devalued. The overall situation, expressed in more familiar if unpalatable terms, is that state schooling at all levels will be required to exercise more social control, engage in further instrumental employment-related functions, and educate less people less well. Its role in promoting traditionally valued liberal cognitive pursuits, and fostering what are commonly regarded as intellectual virtues and excellences, will seriously and markedly decline.

There are two obvious implications for schools and teachers in all of this. First, we will experience a growing two-fold competition for resources. On the one hand, as the overall financing for public schooling decreases the better placed schools will be able to compete more effectively for, and better manage, larger shares of the cake. This means that a more highly stratified state school system will emerge, with the better resourced schools being able to provide greater educative opportunities. And on the other hand parents will approach schooling competitively. Parents who cannot get their children into the better resourced state schools will in all likelihood seek out the private sector, but only those able to afford the fees that sector charges will, of course, be able to 'choose' to take advantage of its offerings. The emergence of a more highly stratified society thus also looms as a real possibility. The second implication is that the traditional role of the teacher-as-educator, especially in the state-school classroom, will also radically change.

Conclusion

Advanced corporate capitalism in a late contractive and deeply recessive phase cannot coexist easily with universal liberal education, because the latter is not well suited to provide the very workforce and system of social and production relations necessary to maintain and further the development of the capitalist mode of production. There is little doubt that our schools and institutions of higher education will continue to produce higher and higher skilled functionaries displaying perhaps inconceivably high levels of intellectual development — but increasingly there will be proportionately fewer of them (and there may also be proportionately less employment opportunities for them, given that government statistics (for example, ABS, 1987) show that while more people are gaining higher educational qualifications, an increasing proportion of them are either out of work and/or on the dole). On the other hand the need for more and continually deskilled productive labour will result in undeveloped and unrealized human potential, and increasingly greater proportional wastage of human resources.

This trend, and the wastage accompanying it, will not be easily stemmed or reversed, even by the most well meaning of teachers. But this does not mean forsaking the attempt to promote and develop the fullest range of human potential or abandoning hopes of achieving universal human liberation. What is required in order to achieve these things is not a more assiduous attempt to implement liberal idealist theory in schools or the creation of societies built on economic rationalist lines, but rather continued refinement of constructions relating to desirable human development, along with fundamental reconstruction of cooperative non-market-oriented social contexts in which human potential could be fully valued and fostered.

What those constructions and contexts will look like cannot be described precisely, as their form will be contingent on and shaped by historical development. But whatever the specific form, its achievement will result basically from human labour, both practical and theoretical; and it is unarguably in the interests of the whole of humanity that the full potentialities of human labour — that is, our potential to learn, to acquire skills and abilities, and to act creatively and constructively — be continually fostered and extended. If we are looking to developing, fostering and extending our human capacity to labour, as well as towards social reconstruction designed to create contexts in which all could develop their life potential, there is surely, notwithstanding the inherent and increasing practical difficulties, a place for schools, and teachers, in all of this.

Notes

1 Unproductive labourers pay taxes too, but that tax revenue by definition is not part of surplus value. Tax revenue to be spent on schooling is not, of course, earmarked according to the status of its contributor, and so even though some must come from the levies on unproductive labourers it is still true to say that the expenditure on schooling comes largely, but not totally, from surplus value.

2 Keeping more at school and university longer, while draining capital further in this area, decreases other government outlays such as unemployment benefits, and so acts as a minor, immediate, highly visible and extremely powerful ideological short-term diversion. It could have long-term effects only if the eventual outcome is, as proposals seem to suggest it will be, increased productive labour.

3 Paul Keating, on television 9 February 1992, and quoted in *The Sydney Morning Herald*, 10 February 1992, p. 1. The reference is to the poem *Clancy of the Overflow* by Australia's great celebrant of the bush, A.B. (Banjo) Paterson. As every Australian schoolchild and ex-schoolchild knows, Clancy has literally turned inward from the commercial city to the bush where, as a drover:

> He sees the vision splendid of the sunlit plains extended,
> And at night the wondrous glory of the everlasting stars.

4 Soon after the completion of this text McDonald's entered into a major sports sponsorship arrangement with NSW schools and teachers were asked, none too subtlely, to promote and support McDonald's in various ways in return. Even more recently proceeds from a Coca Cola drink vending machine in a school have been used to employ a support teacher.

Chapter 4

Choice and Ideology

Introduction

A major aspect of the reactions outlined in chapter 2 related to the issue of 'choice'. Reproduction theory, it will be recalled, hardly appeared to engender confidence regarding the individual's capacity to make choices; while practices of cultural and intellectual imperialism faced the charge of undemocratically privileging some people to make decisions for other people who were allegedly perfectly capable of making good, although in all likelihood different choices for themselves. Throughout the critique there ran a common theme; namely the value of people choosing freely, and for themselves.

I have no quarrel with this in principle, and in fact I would strongly advocate, notwithstanding certain appearances that may emerge at particular points in this book, that a major feature of education and schooling ought to place people in positions where they can make meaningful and beneficial choices regarding their own life circumstances. But if this is to lead to something more than the expression of an ideal it is necessary first to face squarely the matter of how freely people actually do choose. And what much debate in this area rather alarmingly overlooks is that, if the social conditions for making free and autonomous choices (and acting as participating citizens in a democratic society) do not exist in practice, then educational policy advocating autonomy, choice and democratic citizenry is likely to be little more than empty idealist rhetoric. It is far more the case that the actual social conditions in question would have to be brought about and put in place *before* educational policy and practice designed to assist people to exercise choice and engage in democratic participation could result in meaningful, positive realistic outcomes. Schooling and education, then, might have to work along with, and be an active agent in social reconstruction, rather than remain a neutral bystander or be a site where options are laid out without favour. Education promoting autonomy, freedom of choice and democracy may, therefore, also be education entailing social reconstruction — and with teachers giving a lead to the process. But first things first. The matter of choice within a social context requires considerable attention at this point.

Choice and the Ideological Subject

In this and the following sections I want to consider broadly the connection between the formation of consciousness (and thus the propensity for making choices), the propagation of ideology, and the operation of schooling within social formations. As I have argued elsewhere in many places (Harris, 1979 and 1982) I take it that human beings are sociohistoric products whose consciousness is significantly socially-historically determined and formed and mediated by ideology, such that people in different social formations, as well as people within particular social formations, have their options largely structured for them, and are, to a significant if variable extent, impeded from making free and autonomous choices. The capacity for making free autonomous choices may be greater in some social formations than others, but it is never unlimited, and we never have truly or completely free choice. Paradoxically, in contexts where this capacity is not large, arguments that advocate free choice and autonomy could, unwittingly or otherwise, support the maintenance and continuation of the status quo and the political and ideological conditions which stabilize it, in much the same way that arguments advocating centralized institutional controls over education, such as national curricula formulated by government bodies, could provide support for existing stabilizing apparatuses, and thus, regardless of motive or intent, potentially fuel conservative and reactionary fires.

The grounding for the position I am adopting lies in the 'ruling class/ruling ideas' theory developed by Marx and Engels in *The German Ideology*, and more recently elaborated by Althusser. This is a thesis about class consciousness, which claims that in any society the consciousness of the oppressed classes and oppressed groups will be dominated and formed by the ruling class which owns and/or controls the means of production. This 'forming of consciousness' is achieved on the one hand by the operation of agencies or apparatuses controlled by the ruling class (such as the media and schooling) disseminating and legitimating ideology or theoretic production which distorts real relations in order to serve the interests of the ruling class; and on the other hand through elaborate sets of established material practices which 'naturalize' legitimated theory and give the appearance that it fits with real experience. The oppressed are then kept in their state of oppression largely through coming to accept ideological representations as the proper and possibly the only way of representing the real state of affairs. Marx and Engels' classic statement (Tucker, 1972) in this regard is well known, but bears quoting in the context of the position being developed here.

> The ideas of the ruling class are in every epoch the ruling ideas: i.e., the class which is the ruling material force of a society, is at the same time its ruling intellectual force. The class which has the means of material production at its disposal, has control at the same time over the means of mental production ... Insofar, therefore, as they rule as a class and determine the extent and compass of an epoch, it is self-evident that they do this in its whole range, hence among other things rule also as thinkers, as producers of ideas, and regulate the production and distribution of the ideas of their age: thus their ideas are the ruling ideas of the epoch ... (pp. 136–7)

That was written a century and a half ago, at a time when exclusive concentration on class relations and less concern with gender, colour, race and age relations could pass more easily by. Today, although modification appears to be required, the thesis still bears attending to in considering the formation of consciousness within societies. Similarly, Marx's more specific argument in his *Preface to A Contribution to the Critique of Political Economy* (Feuer, 1972, pp. 83–7), namely that consciousness is socio-economically determined and ideologically constituted, retains substantial validity. People as individuals may make choices, but as social products and agents they do not naturally make fully free and autonomous choices, nor are they always well positioned to, because their experience and knowledge of the world is, to a significant extent, mediated by social location and ideology. And, as both Marx and later Althusser have suggested, it is largely through this mediation, or the creation and establishment of complex sets of experience and discourse by ideology (and within some social contexts considerable further domination of consciousness by political oppression) that social structures and economic modes which do not serve the best general interest come to be reproduced rather than radically reconstructed by those whom they do not best serve.

This thesis, perhaps not surprisingly, has had a chequered history.

The liberal-rationalist tradition has rarely taken it seriously, and today it even lacks 'home ground support' given the present unfashionable status that Marxism finds itself in. In the past, however, Marxists have made considerable use of the thesis, first, as its roots would suggest, to develop a theory of ideology, then to establish a related context of structuralism, and more recently to espouse reproduction theories of education. But there has not been a neat flow, let alone acceptance of all these ramifications of the thesis, even among Marxists and Neo-Marxists, and a number of deep divisions have occurred. The theory of ideology in particular reached a moment of significance — some would say its low point — with Althusser, whose work, although closely followed by some, also triggered a major reaction from many others who might otherwise have been thought to have been sympathetic.

The basic problem was that the Marx-Engels/Althusser thesis, with its structuralist basis and its reproductive emphasis, sat badly with those members of oppressed groups who, quite often with considerable justification, regarded their own perceptions as something more than passively adopted misrepresentations of what was really happening in the world; and it sat just as badly with those among the privileged who regarded as anathema any theory which hinted of intellectual imperialism, or which might be seen as supporting a position whereby they, or anybody else, could be taken as knowing what oppressed groups don't know but really need to know. Here was a theory which appeared on the one hand to privilege academic perceptions in particular and to allow that these may have escaped or transcended structural determination, but on the other hand not to respect the judgment, autonomy or cultural roots and heritage of the economically and politically oppressed, whom it then categorized as the intellectually oppressed. It took the working class and other oppressed groups, so its critics maintained, to be passive blotting pads of ruling conceptions rather than vital, generative, culturally productive forces; and through its emphasis on the 'forming' of class consciousness it tended to overlook or downplay the agency of individuals. Added to this, it was depressive, offering little apparent hope or openings for action. It appeared, as one representative critic put it (Bowers, 1984a) 'to nullify the individual as a co-participant in the construction and maintenance of social reality' (p. 366).

Such concerns led directly to criticism of the structuralism that tended to co-exist with the theory of ideology within the thesis. Willis (1977) in one of the more extreme reactions, although over-stating and over-generalizing, did hit the central issues of concern when he claimed that:

> Structuralist theories of reproduction present the dominant ide-
> ology (under which culture is subsumed) as impenetrable . . .
> There are no cracks in the billiard ball smoothness of process.
> All specific contradictions and conflicts are smoothed away in
> the universal reproductive functions of ideology . . . (p. 175)

while Dwyer *et al* (1984) characterized another common set of concerns
in noting that:

> reproduction theory has tended to present a closed system of
> cultural formation which effectively denies the cultural identity
> of the working class . . . on deeper analysis the cultural tradi-
> tions of the working class are stronger and more independent
> than these writers would seem to allow. (pp. 28–9)

Such criticism was, and remains, sharply and clearly damaging, and in
the following section when I detail my own support for the theory
regarding consciousness-formation spelt out above, I shall heed the
criticism that needs attending to while at the same time I shall attempt
to indicate that the damage, while real, is nevertheless qualified. Before
doing this, however, there is a prior matter to consider.

The discussion so far has focussed entirely on infighting and incest
in the academic literature, which may suggest that the debate in question was being carried out only in the halls of academe, and was of
interest only or primarily to academics. That is hardly the case, and it
is, of course, of central importance to consider how the debate impinged
on, and was received and furthered by teachers. Unfortunately, however, little information is available in this regard. Certain suggestions
emerged from the academic literature. Connell *et al* (1982), said of
reproduction theory that it:

> repeatedly implied, and sometimes stated openly, that most
> people could not truly understand what was happening to them.
> It was suggested that they were blinded by ideology (which
> was why they went on reproducing the structures); and that
> only intellectuals who understood proper theory really knew
> what was going on. (p. 28)

and they added: 'the contradiction between democratic purposes and
implicit elitism seems to have been sensed by many teachers'. In similar
vein Gibson (1984) linked his attack on structuralism in general with
teachers' supposed perceptions of 'hard-line Marxism', claiming that:

> the level of the discussion and the drive of the argument are ill-received by most teachers whose preference is for more local, less deterministic analyses ... Few teachers enjoy versions of schooling which cast them and their pupils as little more than puppets in the hands of distant, structural puppet-masters whose control of action, through economic forces, is absolute. Harris' claims that 'the material conditions of existing social relations ... determine what shall be transmitted and how', and his assertion that 'Education ... is controlled by the ruling class, the capitalists, to serve their own interests', fall on deaf ears of teachers faced with the multiple demands and realities of actual classrooms. (p. 110)

The sad fact of the matter, however, is that teachers have few avenues through which they can voice their reactions loudly, widely or representatively, and thus what they really felt is not generally known. But it is doubtful whether teachers did in fact sense the contradiction Connell *et al* spoke of, although Connell does provide minimal evidential support, in contrast to Gibson whose claim is totally unsubstantiated (and dismissively patronizing). What is far less open to doubt is that, in the policy suggestions that accompanied critiques of reproduction theory, teachers were continually told not only that there did exist a contradiction of the sort Connell noted, but also that Marxist, Neo-Marxist and structuralist analyses were too removed from the classroom, too deterministic, too conspiratorial and far-fetched, and too depressing to face. And similarly less open to doubt was that the general line of the critiques in question were not without justification. Some of us did take reproduction theory and structuralism too far at times; and a number of the ideas being floated represented a Paulene effect and needed reining in. Teachers, whether working in their classrooms or undertaking industrial activities, could hardly have failed to have noticed that.

This does not mean, however, that all the critiques got everything right, let alone that they avoided over-reacting themselves; and it was by no means shown that reproduction theory was so terribly misconceived that it had to be abandoned completely. Reproduction theory, represented fairly and fully, did not speak in terms of the 'blinding' Connell identifies; and it had available to it a far better developed theory of ideological formation than its critics, especially academic critics in the field of education, granted it. Academic educational debate was circumscribed and poorly positioned at the time, and tended to overlook and avoid a large and fertile field of discourse which may have better informed it. Having earlier picked up on the issue of 'ideology' and consciousness-formation educational debate strangely then veered away from detailed development of theory and analysis of policy and practice in that area. The work of the Frankfurt School, Mouffe, Ricoeur, Bisseret, Therborn, Larrain, P.Q. Hirst, Foucault and especially Gramsci tended not to be fully acknowledged or incorporated when the time was opportune for doing so. But rather than bemoan that here I want now to set out in some detail one aspect of the theory which was not adequately acknowledged, possibly because it was not adequately spelt out.

Consciousness, Choice and the Ideological Subject

Reproduction theory, along with variants of structuralism, may posit that people are constituted as ideological subjects, but it then hardly claims, or at least should not claim, that they are simultaneously converted into fools, or, to use a term popular with the critics, zombies. It does (or should) respect the judgment, culture and heritage of (say) the working class, but in doing so it also 'places' that knowledge and heritage, and indicates that people generally come to perceive the world largely in the categories available and presented to them as legitimate.[1]

Human beings may be born with the biological capacity to learn and to know, but actual human consciousness is not an a-historical part of our natural make-up. It is socially constructed in a broader historical context. People cannot know what has not as yet been constructed as knowledge, such that in mediaeval times it was difficult to postulate and adequately support a theory that the earth rotates on its axis and revolves around the sun. People (short of having travelled widely) also cannot know or be conscious of knowledge that may have been constructed but which is not part of, or accessible to, their particular society's construction of reality. In this way it is unlikely that tribes living deep in the Amazon basin would have any knowledge of, or interest in, the periodic table of the elements which we are so concerned that our children become aware of. Given this, it makes sense to have some sympathy with the position of, say, whalers two centuries ago, who did not understand, and could not have understood the effects their actions would have had on the global ecosystem. And people are unlikely to know or apply theory which may be part of their overall society's construction of reality but which is continually ridiculed and delegitimated by 'official' sources (as socialism was in the Western world throughout the 'cold war'), or which they themselves have either not met or, lacking experience, education or the necessary theoretic and conceptual fundamentals, cannot understand even when they do meet it. In recognizing this we can understand the difficulty if not the virtual impossibility many people would have in gaining access to understanding and interpreting the broad hidden economic and political agendas underlying the policies of governments such as those headed by Margaret Thatcher or Ronald Reagan without an adequate theoretic base from which to do so. People, even (and perhaps especially) in liberal democracies are, as Chomsky (1988 and 1989) has consistently illustrated, more likely to construct their lives, knowledge and beliefs in terms of the broadly consensual framework promoted and legitimated by the media, the education system and, to use Althusser's terminology, the state's other ideological apparatuses.

None of this consigns people to the 'fool' or 'zombie' category, or makes them totally passive compliant followers of ruling socially constructed theory. People think, question, act critically, and they always have room to manoeuvre. This room, however, is also determined by material conditions within the historical moment, and for a host of varied reasons similarly determined some people will question and manoeuvre more than others. These people need not necessarily be academic intellectuals who 'understand proper theory', of course, but there is a case to be made (and it will be made later) for the specifically privileged place and role of the intellectual and for the role of understanding theory. Suffice it to say at this stage that this room to manoeuvre creates an important place in history and social development for those people who have gained particular knowledge otherwise either maliciously or innocently denied to or absent from the consciousness of others. For instance, to follow up an earlier example, nineteenth century whalers had enough to do in risking their lives to catch the whales that continued to provide for their livelihood, and although they were relatively knowledgeable in the ways of 'taking whale' and had, as a group, developed their own deep 'cultural form', they would have had enormous difficulty recognizing the global ecological effects of their profession — effects that became patently obvious to certain experts or intellectuals who in all likelihood had little knowledge of the practical matters of whaling or the culture of whalers. Similarly, history records the demise of many societies that farmed without the benefit of expert advice regarding the long-term effects of their daily life-providing activities, or that adopted political and economic structures which served immediate needs but which created vulnerabilities to exploitation or conquest that historians or political scientists may have been able to reveal and warn against. There are usually limits to the 'local view' or the 'cultural form', and while 'everyday wisdom' and the body of knowledge built up as 'commonsense' is not to be decried outright there is nothing wrong, and much that is appropriate, in confronting such wisdom and commonsense, which is itself a theoretic position, with the theories and knowledge of relevant wider-seeing experts (which is hardly to imply that those experts always get things right).

That is a point which shall gain much greater prominence in later discussion. Here it might simply be recognized that 'confrontation' is integral rather than alien to social reproduction, and ought similarly be integral to reproduction theory. Social reproduction does not occur as a neat smooth flow but rather can become a more or less messy and contested process. 'Struggle' was a key concept in Marx's formulation and account of the historical process; and as Willis (1977) has more recently indicated:

> Social agents are not passive bearers of ideology, but active appropriators who reproduce existing structures only through struggle, contestation and a partial penetration of those structures.[2] (p. 175)

There is, however, another central point to this which bears considering in some detail. As social agents we may be active appropriators, but given the sociohistorical construction and determination of both our consciousness and the broad parameters of our lifeways, even as active appropriators we are still ideological subjects rather than freely-choosing biological entities. That much is unproblematic and easily recognizable. But what is of central importance yet is less easily recognizable is that part of being an active, appropriating ideological subject is, at least initially, to bear the belief that we are not ideological subjects, and to be open to believe that we act freely and autonomously and not in terms of imposed structures and strictures.

This comes about more from ideological placement than restricted intellectual capacity, for it is a feature of ideology to hide its ideological nature. As Althusser has indicated (1984) 'ideology never says, "I am Ideological" ' (p. 49). An analogy can make this clearer.

We all live on a planet that is moving in at least three different ways at virtually inconceivable speeds. It is hurtling through space along with the rest of our solar system; it orbits the sun; and it is spinning on its axis. Yet we on its surface feel no movement, and in our ordinary everyday experience we see no tangible sign of its movement. We construct our lives as if the earth was still.

There are three major reasons why we fail to notice the movement of the earth. The first is that we are moving with it. We are part of, or within, the very condition of its movement. If we could get off and travel sufficiently far away to be outside that condition, at least some aspects of the movement would become manifestly obvious to us. The second reason is that, in our everyday living, we tend not to undertake the highly specialized observations, usually requiring highly sophisticated equipment, that would reveal aspects of the movement to us. We don't normally spend our days watching pendulums swinging, plotting shadows cast by the sun, pondering the Doppler Effect or measuring the distances from us to the nearer stars which continually change as the earth orbits the sun (but some specialized intellectual experts do). And thirdly, a 'stationary earth' theory not only fits in well enough with our common experience, but it also seems to fit in just as well, if not better, than a 'moving earth' theory. There is an apocryphal story about the philosopher who asked a colleague why mediaeval people thought the sun orbited the earth. The second philosopher mused: 'I suppose because that's how it looked'; to which the first philosopher replied: 'But how would it have looked if it looked as if the sun remained still and the earth rotated?'

Ideology works in a similar sort of way. On the one hand we fail to see the real 'movement' and working of certain social and historical conditions because we ourselves are part of history and are moving within those very conditions. While in theory we can criticize a position either from 'outside' or 'within' its parameters, in practice we can mount critiques of our own ideological status only from 'within' that position. If we could place ourselves outside our sociohistoric conditions we might, from such a privileged position, more easily see the actions of any 'puppet masters' who may be holding strings which determine the conditions in question. Secondly, in our normal everyday living we tend not to seek out the highly specialized data that might offer a different account of aspects of our social and historical conditions that seem well enough accounted for anyway. We usually have neither the time, the need, nor the highly esoteric knowledge and skills to do this — these being luxuries afforded to and enjoyed by (usually professional) intellectuals. And thirdly, everyday appearances tend to confirm prevailing legitimated views and not privilege an alternative and possibly better theory. As an example, here grossly oversimplified, consider the way victims of the current recession can find themselves bearing the blame for it through acceptance of the commonly propagated view that the recession is a result of people having committed the sin of purchasing too many imports. This fits with our experience, given that in many things we are either blameworthy or are becoming accustomed to being portrayed as blameworthy, given that we are consumers, and given that an imbalance of imports (which is easily identified and quantified) does tend to accompany recessions. It fits even easier given that very few of us have much of an idea of how recessions come about, nor do we spend our valuable and otherwise committed time looking for the real key indicators (this makes it relatively easy for a united concerted media to simplify the issue and lay out a set of crude but 'legitimated' indicators). And it fits easier still as we muse about the recession while sitting in front of our Japanese television set on a Malaysian cane lounge, sipping a glass of French red and wearing a T-shirt made in China. But regardless of how well such things fit, or are made to appear to fit, it is anything but the case that people who come to accept such ideological representations are stupid, let alone zombies. It is also anything but the case that experts in the particular area, who can view matters from a wider perspective and/or a different initial position, may not be extremely valuable, and serve an important social purpose, in demystifying and correcting commonly held ideological perceptions.

A major difficulty — one almost bordering on a practical paradox — arises at this point. The first move towards countering or demystifying ideological constructions would be to recognize the nature, and then begin to pick out the details, of one's own (and others') constitution as an ideological subject living within the experiential context of such constructions. This is substantially different from a marine biologist standing 'outside' of the practicality of the whaling situation to highlight issues, such as the wide-ranging effects of the destruction of complete species, which those 'inside' may not see. Demystifying ideological issues requires something like getting off the moving earth in order to see how it really moves and how its movement disguises that very fact for those with a less privileged view. The question that immediately arises is how, if we live in ideology, can anyone step outside it to obtain what they claim to be a privileged view? Marx and Engels' 'ruling class–ruling ideas' thesis has often been proclaimed as wrong, self-contradictory or self-defeating on the grounds that, according to the thesis itself, Marx and Engels should have been ideological subjects accepting ruling ideas and thus could not have proposed the thesis in the first place; and Chomsky has often been asked how he is able to not only escape the very persuasiveness of the media which he is subjected to more than most people, but also identify and detail the effects which others fall victim to. I shall indicate later that Gramsci's identification of organic intellectuals — people whose background and life experience lies *within* ideological representations and constructions of experience but whose intellectual and theoretical development places them particularly well, not to escape or appropriate such experience, but to see and evaluate it from *outside* or from a broader context — serves significantly to resolve both the paradox here encountered, as well as many of the problems involved regarding people with more privileged viewpoints intervening in the lives of other people.

Conclusion

Demystification of the process of consciousness-formation, the operation of ideology, the social conditions for choice, and in fact anything regarding the interrelation of society, schooling and education will not be self-generating; and it is unfortunate that the above-quoted critics of structuralism and reproduction theory fail to give sufficiently plausible indications of how such a process could reasonably happen. On the other hand, however, they do not categorically deny the teacher or intellectual a prominent role of some sort in the educative agenda. The result, as I see it, is that they tend to set teachers swimming relatively aimlessly in a sea of non-intervention or unspecific intervention; which would be consistent with their own attempt to avoid taking an interventionist stance lest they find themselves hoisted on that petard of their own making. But if intervention does raise that danger, it does not necessarily follow that the danger must be avoided. Being hoisted may be uncomfortable, but, along with concentrating the mind, it places one in a position where potentially one can see further. The task is to remain conscious and to continue the struggle from a different plane.

If a process of demystification is to be initiated and propelled then human agency is required. If the process is to be genuine demystification then the agents involved will be agitators. If a beginning is envisaged then, in the current parlance of some, we would be looking to 'proactive agency'; and proactive agency is nothing other than taking a vanguard role. There is sad irony in finding this promising conclusion and tactic, which oddly tends to stick in the throat of much radical discourse, emerging from a field of rhetoric that is currently one of the leading candidates for demystification.

I shall argue later that teachers could be well placed to demystify and lay bare the sorts of contradictions and sociohistorically legitimated constructions I have spoken of, and, to pick up earlier points, who would also be well placed to restructure and reorientate schooling for the purpose of rational social reconstruction, and, through gaining control of the curriculum, to educate the young to participate in the future exercise and control of genuine democratic political power. In doing so, as I shall indicate, teachers will have to devise ways of acting in a counter-hegemonic manner whilst working within a material ideological context, and they will also have to recognize and significantly transcend their own ideological constitution whilst living within the context that brings about that constitution in the first place. But it is not quite set up. There is more that has to be said about justifying teacher-intervention in both the lives of individuals and in social reconstruction.

Notes

1 Connell himself clearly recognizes this where it suits his argument. For instance he states (Dwyer *et al*, 1984) that:

> It is plain that the mass of people accept the socioeconomic system of capitalism as the normal and natural condition of life; alternatives are seen as exotic, alien and often threatening. Their chief hopes are for private fulfilment, in a family context, and personal success in work, sex and social relations. In a limited sense capitalism delivers the goods . . . Working men and women do not commonly identify their fate with that of a whole class, nor do they have effective ways in which a class interest in the transformation of society can be assured. (p. 32)

2 Willis's statement is intended, in context, as a critique of structuralism in general and Althusser in particular. It seems to me, however, to be more a spelling-out of a sophisticated structuralist position than a critique. Willis, along with many others, also seems to have overlooked Althusser's repeated assertion (1984, p. 21 and pp. 58–9) that the 'Ideological State Apparatuses' he categorized are conflict-ridden confrontational sites and stakes of struggle.

Chapter 5

Justifying Teacher Intervention

Introduction

In the preceding chapters I have outlined traditional idealist approaches to education, along with certain contemporary economic rationalist proposals regarding restructuring schooling and the provision of education, and I have indicated the broad nature as well as some of the details of my opposition to these programs. I have also noted recent reactions to the idealist and essentialist proposals that schools should engage primarily in transmitting liberal studies of the sort Arnold called 'the best that has been thought and said in the world', which numerous critics have seen variously as a form of intellectual imperialism perpetuating elements of ruling class culture and oppression, as unconnected and irrelevant to the real needs of the majority of the populace, and as politically conservative and reactionary in terms of their place in reinforcing existing social relations. I have indicated further the conflicting counter-arguments proposed that schools and teachers should focus on the real needs and interests of the working class and/or the oppressed; that teachers might ply their knowledge and values to the end of improving the lot of their pupils but that neither they nor schools have the right or the duty to actively promote or engage in social reconstruction; and that teachers might leave well enough alone given that they do not necessarily understand working-class experience or know what is best for oppressed groups, nor are they necessarily bearers of knowledge, values and programs of action superior to that borne by their charges.

In the face of both this vigorous conflict of ideas and the contemporary process of proletarianization and deprofessionalizing teachers, I now want to put a specific case for teachers learning, guarding, preserving, fostering and transmitting the most valuable manifestations of human achievement and capability and, at the same time, promoting rational social reconstruction. What I am looking to envisages teachers being deeply involved in decision-making with regard to the content and value of the substantive curriculum they are to control and transmit, and with regard to forms of social relations and conditions that might well be sought and constructed. I shall argue that teacher intervention in the lives of the younger generation can be justified on non-idealist and non-imperialist lines, that the curricula involved can be justified on non-essentialist grounds, and that teachers of a certain sort would be well placed to engage in, rather than retreat from, activities directed towards social reconstruction. I shall show that teachers armed with a curriculum not totally dissimilar to traditional liberal curricula are not necessarily enemies of the oppressed, that the transmission of valuable manifestations of human achievement and the quest for rational social reconstruction are compatible and anything but conflicting activities, and that rather than merely collaborate in forms of intercultural articulation, teachers are in fact well placed to lead in the task of social reconstruction.

Schooling, Democracy, Autonomy and Social Reconstruction

Given that so much of this book is concerned with teachers taking a vanguard role in rational social reconstruction, it might reasonably be enquired as to what form of social reconstruction is being sought. Anyone expecting a plea for a classless society ruled by a dictatorship of the proletariat, at a time when such a thing is politically unfeasible, ideologically unpalatable and historically impossible, may be disillusioned to find that I seek nothing more than a form of democratic socialism in which all citizens have equal rights and who, as autonomous agents, have equal potential and genuine opportunity to exercise their rights and to participate in the exercise and control of political power.

That, on the face of it, may seem both unremarkable and little if anything removed from the proposals of liberal rationalism. Within that particular tradition democracies are commonly characterized as social formations in which people not only have rights as citizens, but have pretty much equal rights and equal power and opportunity to exercise those rights. John White (1988) spells out these sentiments a little more fully when he says that 'Every citizen in a democracy . . . should have an equal right to participate in the control or exercise of political power' (p. 220), and he then links the task of government in liberal democratic societies with education thus:

> In a liberal-democratic society the proper task of government is to promote the well-being of all citizens by equipping them with the necessary conditions of an autonomous life. Educationally, this means helping to build up in them those dispositions and forms of understanding which are required for autonomy. (*ibid*, pp 229–30)

White claims that a minimum test of a curriculum's commitment to democratic principles 'is whether it includes among its goals preparing all young people to become equal citizens of a democracy'; and that not least among these principles is 'equality of political power' (*ibid*, p. 220).

The problem with this, and it is symptomatic of much idealist and liberal writing on education, is that it first reifies and 'assumes' democracy (in much the same way that 'the future' is commonly reified as an entity lying somewhere out in front of us patiently and passively waiting for us to make our way to it) and having done that it then argues for education to assist with bringing about things such as autonomy which are deemed desirable in a democracy and necessary for its continuation.

The reality of the situation, however, is that schooling can effectively prepare all its charges to become participating citizens, and build up the dispositions required for democratic participation, only within social formations which actually allow for, and which will actively promote, participatory democracy and the equal rights of all citizens. This state of affairs will not, of course, be found in fascist regimes. And although rationalizations might prevail, they will similarly not be found within exploitative social relations; whether these be of a crude socialist sort founded on political and ideological oppression and the propagation of unquestioned party or other dogma, or of a capitalist sort founded on a form of economic exploitation which results in some, the rich, holding and maintaining power largely because many are rendered both poor *and* oppressed.[1] If 'preparing all young people to become equal citizens of a democracy' is to be a serious aim of education indicating more than pointless or hopeful preparation, there must exist social conditions within which democratic participation can genuinely occur. To speak of such preparation or, *pace* Walker, of maximizing people's opportunities 'to determine their own destinies' within a structural context wherein such opportunity cannot realistically exist is, if not to embrace idealism then at the least to engage in hollow rhetoric. If these opportunities do not prevail then a precondition for seriously holding such an educational aim would be to construct the social conditions in which the required participation could be realized (and then historically to continually reconstruct social conditions encouraging and facilitating such opportunity and participation).

Much the same can be said about the idealist tendency to reify and 'assume' autonomy. Autonomy is not an essentialist 'form' that can be abstracted from people's material conditions of existence. We might reasonably discuss the meaning or conditions of 'autonomy' abstractly, but we cannot seriously and sensibly propose, in practical policy-orientated terms, developing autonomous people or treating students as responsible autonomous individuals, outside of a social context in which autonomous people can exist and be fostered. So, as with democratic participation, if autonomy is to be realizable as an aim of education, there must exist social conditions within which people can act as autonomous agents. If these do not prevail at any time or place, then a precondition for having autonomy as a serious realizable educational aim would be to construct such conditions. And since a central condition for the development and fostering of autonomy is the existence of social relations based on equity and equality, it would appear that education seeking to produce autonomous agents might actively promote consciousness and practices directed towards empowering people to bring about such social relations. That end, encompassable *within* the notion of 'planning pupils' futures', is worthwhile, defensible, and unarguably, although not necessarily uniquely, fundamental.

The preceding discussion serves to distinguish my position from liberal rationalism and liberal idealism even though there might be agreement, at one level, regarding the desirability of having all people participate autonomously in democratic processes within society. In common with modern liberalism I take it that schooling, and of course the curriculum, should prepare all to become participating citizens of a democracy; and that education should be centrally although not exclusively directed to equipping all educands to lead an autonomous life. But in order to ground that imperative (which might otherwise be nothing more than a pious hope) in material reality I take it to be part of the role of schooling and teachers to engage in and give a lead to forms of social reconstruction necessary to bring about the material conditions in which people really can act as autonomous democratic citizens. It is not my intention here to explore specific details regarding the role of schooling in such social reconstruction, since much of that would be historically determined, but two general matters bear some elaboration at this point.

First, schools are, on one very significant dimension, unlikely and potentially contradictory places to prepare students for participatory democracy. Not only are schools (at least as we commonly know them) not democracies themselves, but also a large number of their practices are a long way removed from those usually regarded as democratic. This has led some to advocate forms of democratization of schooling, to promote significant extensions of children's rights, freedoms and actions within schools, and to champion issues such as equality in decision-making across the school. I am not supportive of that position in general. Rather, I would want to maintain that in particular specific areas, especially those concerning formulation of the curriculum and assessment, it is appropriate that certain broad democratic practices and principles, such as those relating to equality among participants and majority decision-making, are largely overridden and removed. As I shall argue in the following chapters there are, given checks and caveats, certain things within schooling which should be the province of teachers, and central among these are determination of the curriculum and assessment of its mastery. This means that for pupils, as future citizens, a first or early step, and a long continuing one in learning to participate in democratic processes and in building up the dispositions required for autonomy, is to engage with and attempt to master a largely, but not necessarily totally imposed curriculum. This also has to be done within the constraints, or hidden curriculum, associated with formal schooling, and hopefully pupils might eventually come to understand, rather than merely suffer, both. It means also that teachers have to be prepared to intervene, not as cultural imperialists or uncritical promulgators of their favourite subject and bits of knowledge, but rather towards the end of producing informed, critical thinkers; and to do so with a well-developed understanding of the real and pseudo-conflicts involved in the schooling process, and with the ability to justify the complex issues entailed in the educative endeavour. Here, then, lies a major paradox and practical problem confronting teachers: in the very promotion of social reconstruction towards democracy they have to engage in certain non-democratic practices.

Secondly, although schooling functions roughly in the form indicated by Althusser as an ideological state apparatus serving to secure the reproduction of the relations of production, or to put it more gently, as an agent of social conservation, neither the thought nor the practice of social reconstruction need be given up by default. Schooling itself is a central agency in the dynamics of history; and notwithstanding the very real and powerful structural constraints and political conditions that impinge on schooling, it is in the hands of both those who control and who operate schools to determine, to a significant extent (which is itself dependent on the specific conditions of the historical moment in question) whether, and how far, schools are to conserve or challenge the existing social order. There is thus always at least the potential, if not more, for teachers (among others, and especially *with* others) to work towards the construction of democratic forms even within fundamentally non-democratic contexts. This now highlights a second major paradox and practical problem, at least for those teachers working within contexts of economic and/or political exploitation that are otherwise termed liberal democracies. In order to promote social reconstruction they must pose and confront as a problem both the schools and the very context that structures the schools within which they work. And as they may also have to confront their own professional being as a problem, along with the knowledge they convey, they might well not expect an easy passage.

Teachers are not exempt from being constituted as ideological subjects, and their knowledge and consciousness is as much socially constructed as anybody else's. Therefore, in order to successfully engage with the paradoxes and problems they will encounter in engaging in the sort of endeavour I am proposing, teachers will have need of the skills and a knowledge-base by means of which they can become reflexively aware and recognize and understand the operation of ideology and the process of the social formation of consciousness. To this end a strong critical basis in theory, which Smith (1992) has nicely called 'an entitlement to understanding', along with grounding in at least sociology and philosophy, as well as other human sciences, may not go astray. It is worth noting at this stage that expanding the knowledge-base of teachers in the manner indicated above potentially better fits them as organic intellectuals in the Gramscian sense to be outlined in chapter 7, and it also has the potential to make them critical of both the knowledge-base and the social-historical location of traditional intellectuals, as well as to promote awareness of the hegemonic processes of the state. It can therefore be seen to be in the interests of the state (as a repressive conservative body seeking to preserve dominant and ruling interests) to deny such a knowledge-base to teachers; which may have something to do with contemporary moves to delegitimate educational theory and critical study of the social sciences in teacher-education programs and to relocate much of initial teacher education in schools rather than universities.

Towards a Justification of Committed Intervention: A Negative Case

Before I begin to build a positive case for active teacher-intervention I shall lay some of the groundwork necessary by first countering the major arguments so far noted against teachers having control of curriculum and using that control, along with professional privilege and power, to determine notions of the good life and to point future generations in particular directions and towards particular social constructions. I shall begin this exercise somewhat obliquely by first considering the idealist proposals that curricula ought be chosen and determined on epistemological criteria, and that there is a core of essential knowledge which all pupils should encounter and engage with.

Beyond Essentialism

Given that the period of formal schooling is temporally finite, and that curricula have to be selected from an infinite body of knowledge, those concerned with such selection implicitly ask Herbert Spencer's question: 'What knowledge is of most worth?' (Spencer, 1963, 1–44).[2] They might disagree about the substantive content they seek to include, but they all give the very clear impression that they believe the particular knowledge they champion is justifiably privileged for inclusion in a finite and severely limited curriculum. Spencer himself wanted education based on and around science; Matthew Arnold countered with a case for the humanities, and particularly 'letters', providing the core of a curriculum eventually concerned with the 'entire circle of knowledge'; M.V.C. Jeffreys envisaged a religious centre for education; F.R. Leavis saw literary criticism as the central discipline best capable of sensitizing the learner to approach other studies; R.M. Hutchins and Mortimer Adler, and now Bloom, sought education based on readings of the 'Great Books'; Herbert Read promoted education based on art; the Harvard Report, 'General Education in a Free Society' (Harvard University, 1945) identified logical, relational and imaginative modes of thinking which it then claimed education should develop; A.D.C. Peterson (1960) identified four modes of experience — logical, moral, empirical and aesthetic — which education should foster; Ernst Cassirer and P.H. Phenix put forward other particular modes; L.A. Reid (1961) championed his 'ways of knowledge and experience'; Michael Oakeshott (1967) wanted education to tune into the voices of practical activity, science, poetry and history; and figuring prominently in recent debate P.H. Hirst (1974) saw liberal education as the development of mind, which in turn was allegedly initiation into forms of knowledge that have become differentiated out over human history.

In at least all but one of the above cases the Spencerian question has been addressed from an idealist and essentialist perspective, and has been contextualized within epistemology and metaphysics. Now the fact that there is such widespread disagreement as to what knowledge is of most worth from *among* those who believe in the first place that there is a body of essential knowledge which ought to have a privileged place in educational curricula, does not constitute a definitive case against essentialism. It does, however, indicate that the bases some essentialists use to determine their privileged content may be incommensurate with those used by other essentialists (some, for instance, look to 'subjects' while others look to 'ways of thinking'), and it shows even more significantly that essentialists tend to ground their reasons for choice of content in terms of 'external' criteria. The knowledge championed more often than not tends to emerge not through any justification of its intrinsic essential value, but rather as something seen to be instrumental towards achieving particular favoured ends (and at times even as a parade of the proposer's favourite pass-times); and to date no pure essentialist argument has satisfactorily been made. This historical situation has, in fact, tended to support the compelling anti-essentialist position put forward in antiquity by Aristotle in his *Politics* and *Ethics*; namely that curricula decisions and conclusions regarding what is to be studied, by whom, and to what extent, must derive from premises other than epistemological ones. Epistemological theories are simply neither necessary nor sufficient to establish conclusions about what knowledge is worthwhile in general, let alone to establish conclusions about the content of education or about what knowledge shall be granted formal privilege for transmission and legitimation in any society (as, for example, in the school curriculum). Epistemology may raise issues relevant to formulating answers to such questions; but even the merest materialist consideration reveals that the provision of formal schooling, along with its curriculum, is politically determined. Education systems may be charged with transmitting knowledge, but they do this neither in a metaphysical realm nor in a mystical epistemological context. Such transmission occurs basically, fundamentally and only within the material conditions of existing social relations: and education, almost in contrast to what idealist epistemologists proclaim, is a major factor in the production and legitimation of certain kinds of knowledge which serve particular interests in particular societies. It is thus first and foremost a political act, and never a pure application of essentialist epistemological theory (Harris, 1979, pp. 137–64; Apple, 1992b).

But if education is a political act, and if epistemological theories are neither necessary nor sufficient to establish conclusions about the content of education, the question of choice still remains. I shall leave positive points regarding this till later and here remain in a negative mode, noting simply two things. First, teachers are hardly bound by rational criteria to accept and transmit curricula allegedly determined on essentialist and/or epistemological grounds. Secondly, if 'someone' is determining curricula on political grounds then there is surely an opening here for making a case that teachers ought to have a privileged place in this political process.

Beyond Liberalism

I want to turn now from epistemology to social philosophy, and in that context consider and counter three issues that commonly emerge from liberalism, and all of which are conveniently found in John White's position as outlined earlier.

The first of these issues is the notion that questions about the aims and broad content of education, being concerned with the kind of society we wish to live in, are political questions; and as such within a democracy they should be resolved not by privileged and/or elite bodies but rather by the citizenry as a whole. That conclusion may express popular sentiments, but it should be noted that, for all its popularity, it neither holds nor follows unproblematically. It is simply not the case, logically or any which-way, (and notwithstanding the dubious suppressed premises which tend to be hidden within the formulation of such a position) that in a democracy political questions are necessarily to be resolved by the citizenry as a whole.

This may actually be a disguised blessing for liberalism. If the position is accepted as following it then becomes necessary to identify the 'citizenry as a whole' or the 'public', and to identify the relation between these bodies (or this body) and the government which is usually charged with representing them. Such identification often leads to rather strained proposals. For instance, White's liberal anti-elitist position forbids education from being spoken for specifically by professional educational experts such as teachers, yet allows somehow that it is both proper and correct that the views of the 'citizenry as a whole' on education be represented by members of political parties who first happen to win preselection to seats and then gain popular majorities at election time, regardless of their knowledge of educational issues. In contemporary practice dominated by party politics decision by parliamentary representatives is a weird aberration of the idea of having the people themselves setting the educational (or any) agenda. Most importantly, however, neither an anti-elitist position, nor the idea that political questions require resolution by the citizenry as a whole, establishes that a privileged voice should not be given in specific areas to recognized experts in those areas. Once again we find an opening for a case to be made for privileging teachers in this political process.

Secondly, it is a cornerstone of liberalism, and one specifically laid by White (1988), that the curriculum should 'aim at acquainting pupils impartially with a whole range of different ideals of the good life' (p. 224). However, since the range that might be offered for acquaintance within a prescribed curriculum cannot be infinite, it must itself be selected. This requires that we ask a variation of Spencer's question, namely what ideals are most worth acquainting pupils with? — and consequently that choices and selections be made from within the 'whole range' of ideals of the good life. At this point two further questions arise; namely who shall make these choices, and on what grounds? These are questions liberalism becomes absurdly hoisted on, having disbarred both government and specific experts from having a privileged voice in addressing them. Yet again an opening appears for, or is literally handed to, those who might seek to stake a claim for teachers.

Finally, it might well be recognized that liberalism itself is internally contradictory in that, contrary to its own principles and dictates, it itself privileges a certain view of the good life over others. It is thus open to contest and challenge rather than uncritical acceptance, and there is no rational reason why teachers (or anyone) ought to feel committed to its premises or bound by its conclusions in this particular area.

Beyond Promoting Choice Through Cultural Articulation

I noted earlier the position put by Jim Walker (1988) regarding 'cultural articulation', in which it was declared that 'the search for common ground is the only way of pursuing equitably the welfare of different groups and individuals' (p. 157), and which advocated seeking common ground, promoting choice and the expansion of options as the basis for schooling and teaching. I shall now set out aspects of that position a little more fully and, given that it is as sophisticated a case as one is likely to find in its area, I shall subject it to particular attention which, perhaps paradoxically and contrary to Walker's thrust, will then open up further spaces for teacher action.

With regard to the matter of choice Walker recognizes that not all choices or choosers are equally powerful, that in certain circumstances people's choices may all be unpleasant, and that people are not equal in exercising options nor can they always create their own options. He further recognizes that:

> Since choices are made from among options, and options are always to some extent given, to ignore the options is to miss the structure of social power. This structure means that some people's choices are privileged, often at the expense of others. (*ibid*, p. 96)

However, when it comes to policy recommendations neither the recognized structural barriers and constraints nor the general principles of equity and equality are given primacy, and Walker puts consideration and adaptation to existing concrete conditions for choice above attempting to create better social conditions. He concludes:

> An overriding issue for educational philosophy and policy is the determination of equity of opportunity and outcome in actual, concrete conditions of choice. This . . . requires recognition that the relevant choices are *cultural.* Individuals cannot be simply severed from their cultures, though they can change. Unless cultures are running against the common interest of the community, which includes the protection of the rights of individuals within the community, individuals may choose options lower as well as higher in the socioeconomic scale. These may or may not be best for them, but it is up to them, not educators or policy makers, to judge what is good for them. (*ibid*, pp. 169–70)

Walker sees the development of responsible and autonomous individuals who are capable of judging for themselves as a 'fundamental educational principle', to be overridden only by education for the common good. He states (1988) that, rather than base policy and practice on equality of outcome or opportunity, we would do better to apply the criterion:

> what, consistent with the common good, *maximizes* the opportunity for *these* pupils to determine their own destinies? What options can be made available to them given their background and, more importantly, given the problems they presently face,

as they see them and in line of development from their currently understood options? (p. 170)

This position raises a number of problems revolving around the 'common interests' of the 'community'; such as how the former might relate to the frequently cited 'common good criteria' and, as is so often the case in such discussions, what exactly is meant by 'community'.[3] But a more significant set of problems is raised by the position taken on choices, potential and perception. First, Walker accepts that choice and potential are rooted in present existing opportunities, and he proposes that educational and other policy be contextualized within that framework — which is cold comfort for the structurally disadvantaged, chilly in proportion to their existing level of structural disadvantage (and fairly cruel and denying of hope for the commonly identified growing underclass). Secondly, Walker declares that people should be allowed to judge for themselves even if they judge badly. (This seems to negate the very *raison d'être* of a teaching force, and even educational policy-making itself, unless all is to be consigned to ways and means of laying out options.) And finally he states that options are to be made available 'given the problems [people] presently face, as they see them . . .' It is thus accepted that people can be structurally disadvantaged, and that they can choose badly; yet it is still advocated that educational policy and provision be predicated on people's own perceptions of their problems — which may be poor perceptions, or even misperceptions of what the real problems are. So, even while recognizing structural disadvantage, and that some choices can be bad and some perceptions can be poor or even wrong, Walker must, if he is to be consistent, oppose intervention in the form of promoting more informed and/or preferable judgments on the assumption that it is better to maximize people's opportunity to determine their own destiny.

Four points can now be made. First, this position, as any number of examples could show, runs the patent risk of turning non-intervention into a potentially harmful mode of operation. To give one example: many people see their own very real personal problem of being unemployed as having been caused by gender and racial groups (women and 'blacks') taking the available jobs, and see as real and proper solutions returning women to the kitchen and 'blacks' to 'where they came from'. It is difficult, from the context of Walker's position, to find grounds for intervening in situations and actions based in such perceptions. Secondly, Walker talks about 'a wise approach to curriculum'; yet given the thrust of his argument it is difficult to see who might justifiably determine and judge, or even be authorized to determine and judge, what is wise with regard to curriculum. Thirdly, although correctly noting that people cannot be easily severed from their culture, Walker fails to establish that the search for common ground is 'the only way' to equitably pursue the welfare of different groups and individuals. And finally the overall position taken fails to recognize that 'enhancing the freedom and power of pupils to make personally fulfilling and socially beneficial choices about how to live their lives' might actually require the prior or simultaneous transformation or reconstruction of the social system itself. On all four counts, whether Walker would welcome it or not, there is space for teacher intervention. And if we now add some aversion to simply sitting back and allowing people to judge badly and to choose what may not be best for themselves, a fifth count quickly emerges.

Notes

1　This is a horse which is alive and kicking and which must continue to be flogged. It is timely to see Colin Lankshear consistently building the theme into his *Literacy, Schooling and Revolution* (1987) and Hugh Lauder deliberately calling attention to it in 'The New Right Revolution and Education in New Zealand' in Middleton, Codd and Jones (1990, p. 24).
2　Underlying this question, as Apple and Christian-Smith have noted (1991) is the more contentious question: 'whose knowledge is of most worth?' (p. 1).
3　For excellent discussion on this point see Peters and Marshall (1988).

Chapter 6

Teachers and Committed Intervention

Introduction

In the previous chapter I have argued that there is insufficient in idealist epistemology, or in liberal theory, or in the broad theory of cultural articulation to necessarily put paid to a case for teachers having greater control of schooling and curricula, nor for inveighing against teachers directing such increased control towards the end of social reconstruction. In fact I have shown how deficiencies in each of the programs considered serve to indicate and highlight spaces and directions for teachers to work in. It remains now to build a positive case for active teacher-intervention, and so I shall proceed to put in place some of the foundations and the pillars on which that case will be built. I shall consider first the legitimacy of ideologically-based politically committed discourse, enquiry and practice, and thus the legitimacy of offering substantive proposals for social change. I shall then, while harking back to earlier discussion regarding the social formation of consciousness, consider the role of teachers with special regard to the relation between intervention and empowering.

The Legitimation of Non-neutrality

A strong justification for the production of ideologically based and politically committed discourse and research, as well as for undertaking politically committed educational practice, can be found in recent developments in philosophy and social theory, especially as they focus on and relate to science and the social sciences, including sociology and education.

The continued attack on essentialist and foundational views of knowledge, the collapse of the fact/value distinction, the establishment of the theory-ladenness of observations thesis and the recognition that all discourse and research is political, non-neutral and theory dependent, have together constituted a definitive critique of the idealist and positivist traditions that have underpinned and dominated the historical development of the human and social sciences, including education. Notwithstanding the lingering effects and pressures of the 'hand of the past', discourse regarding epistemological, theoretical, and methodological issues in the human sciences is being reshaped within programs such as materialism, post-positivism and post-modernism, and continued challenges are being made with regard to the matters of justification, understanding and even knowledge itself.

In this process a number of things have been sufficiently well established, even if they are not always fully acknowledged by those holding to idealist and positivist positions. The notions of neutrality and objectivity in social science and education have been revealed as myths which, among other things, mystified the inherently ideological nature of educational practice and of discourse and research in the human sciences, and which also legitimated privilege based on class, colour, race and gender. The recognition that the achievement of pure scientific reason and value-neutral social science were unrealizable, deceptive and false hopes has facilitated and lent respectability to the production and application of consciously political and social reason. And the increasingly common shift away from conceptualizing a given world 'out there' waiting to be found, read and known as it really is, and towards recognition of the notion of constructed worlds, has led to a deepened understanding of the way human beings construct knowledge of their world, along with its history, through their actual experience of economic, social and political relations and conditions in that world.

This is not to say, of course, that there has been universal acceptance of 'self-confessed' ideological value-based research and practice, or that there are not those remaining who still regard traditional concepts of objectivity as both possible and desirable in the human and social sciences. However, the potential and the justification for such a reorientation certainly now exists; and within such a reoriented framework discourse, theory, research and practice which is openly value-based can be clearly recognized as being neither more nor less ideological and political than was mainstream, allegedly neutral, positivism. Thus a legitimate question and approach now confronting those involved with the human and social sciences, including researchers and educators, is one that states and governments have always had little problem in posing and addressing — namely not how best to strive to be neutral or objective (in the sense of being disinterested), but rather what to be committed to. As Lather (1986a) has stated:

> Once we recognize that just as there is no neutral education there is no neutral research, we no longer need apologize for unabashedly ideological research and its open commitment to using research to criticize and change the status quo. (p. 67)

To this there can be added a conclusion which is fundamentally diffe-rent from that derivable from liberal rationalism's recognition of the politi-cal nature of education: namely that we also no longer need apologize for unabashedly ideological education (which state authorities have always employed but hardly rush to apologize for), nor for an open political commitment to using education to criticize the status quo, or even for attempting to change the status quo should such change be rationally defensible. From a post-positivist perspective, as well as from anti-positivist and/or materialist perspectives, a politically committed approach to research on education, to educational practice and to for-mulating and transmitting substantive curricular content, is not unjustifiable.

It should be stressed immediately, however, that the position out-lined above does not necessarily open a particular set of important floodgates. Acceptance of the defensibility of political commitment, and with that the recognition that commitment and intervention in teaching and research is similarly potentially defensible, does not lead inexorably to the conclusion that commitment *per se* is necessarily good and so provide universal licence for anyone and everyone to become totally unabashed and intervene at will, or by any means. Neither does it indicate that all views and/or value judgments are, from a rational point of view, equally acceptable, and so throw open the doors leading to relativism. And finally, if not exhaustively, it by no means establishes the unwelcome possibility that ends in themselves can justify means. Underlying the whole of this position there still remains the obligation for justification. What have changed and shifted are the objects and focus of that justification.

Once ideologically committed research, discourse, policy formation and teaching are recognized as being, on the grounds indicated above, in themselves neither more nor less neutral and scientific than the ide-alist and positivist models respectively (not to mention the economic rationalist model), it emerges that what requires justification is not some 'neutral', 'a-political', 'formal' or 'scientific' basis of any enquiry and/or action at hand, but rather the issues and ends the enquiry or action is directed and committed to. For example, we need not shy away from, or apologize for, undertaking research or engaging in teaching that challenges the status quo in order to contribute to constructing a more egalitarian social order, provided that we can rationally demonstrate deficiencies within the status quo and justify the quest for a more egalitarian social order. It is the ends or purposes which, in the first instance, and not exclusively, must be defensible, and need to be defended.

Teachers, Intervention and Empowerment

With the question of neutrality and ideological commitment behind us it is now time to consider a positive case with regard to teachers intervening in children's lives and engaging in rational social reconstruction. I shall therefore now indicate the pillars on which my own position regarding the role of teachers is built.

My case is premised on open support for a particular form of intervention directed towards rational social reconstruction. Given what I have said in chapter 4 about ideology and consciousness formation it should come as no surprise that, rather than accept and promote a version of Marxism that intimates that the oppressed can, unaided, engage in a form of self-liberation, I shall, following Gramsci, argue instead for encouraging those who have established informed positions and privileged perspectives for themselves to intervene, where appropriate, in assisting the liberation and empowerment of others. In doing so I shall be promoting a version of structuralist materialism and at the same time exploiting certain tensions between the structuralism involved and the notion of schooling functioning as a liberating agency with teachers acting in part as political activists within their schools.

The tensions I speak of have often been pointed to as a problem or a weakness in Marxist theory, and even as potentially capable of negating liberating practices. They need not, in fact, be anything of the kind.

A Marxist view of education should be particularly aware of and sensitive to tensions within the provision and practice of schooling and education. Schools would be immediately regarded as a prime site for tension, given that they are provided by the state to conserve and stabilize a status quo that particularly favours the interests and needs of the ruling class, and yet could be staffed by people and/or influenced by parents who may have quite opposing purposes and interests in mind, and be populated by pupils who may not readily and passively accept being formed into particular types of ideological subjects. Marxism would also recognize the tensions inherent in a social system which on the one hand develops class consciousness amongst the oppressed through their daily experience of class relations, but seeks on the other hand to both mystify and eclipse such consciousness through the operation of its formal agencies or state apparatuses, such as schooling. Further, Marxism would recognize rather than be troubled by the fact that bourgeois individualism is in tension with, rather than the manifestation of, individual autonomy. Marxism also recognizes that there is space for pupil autonomy, which is hardly an all-or-nothing affair, to grow and be fostered within schools, just as there is also space in schools for teaching directed towards social reconstruction. And at the more theoretical level there is also space and potential within the context of structuralism to recognize schooling as a potential liberating agency rather than something which necessarily, universally and unfailingly operates in a closed and oppressive form. There is, in fact, no contradiction in both adopting the form of structuralism in which this overall argument is situated and in identifying schooling's potential to liberate people from ignorance and impotency,[1] let alone with seeing the liberating potential of schooling intimately related to teachers having greatly increased control over matters such as curricula, as well as with teachers actively intervening in order to empower and equip new generations with tools potentially useful for their liberation. What we might find, of course, is *increased* tensions within schooling which both serves the state and seeks to promote its overthrow as an oppressive body. Similarly, there may be increases in existing tensions when liberal education is wrenched from a form of liberalism which constitutes particular types of ideological subjects, to *liberating* education which develops autonomous individuals capable of constructing and perpetuating a genuine participatory democracy. All of these tensions can usefully be exploited.

With that at least indicated the stage might now be better set for further considering the issues of intervention and empowerment in teaching. It is, however, a stage still dominated by a major remaining tension, namely that created by the very coupling of 'intervention' with 'empowering'; or the tension between, on the one hand, intervening in people's lives in order to direct their choices and actions towards particular ends, and on the other hand seeking to empower those people to be able, on their own account, to make meaningful and worthwhile choices and decisions regarding their own lives. Quite often this particular tension is avoided rather than resolved by stepping back from intervention on the grounds that intervention in any guise is a form of imperialism and is thus always anything but empowering. This reaction,

I believe, is mistaken and misconceived in that it fails to take adequate note of the social construction of consciousness and the constitution of ideological subjects within society. Aversion to intervention in material terms is not a matter of keeping oneself out of an ongoing process in which people continually choose freely and autonomously, but rather failure to react to, or intervene in, a social process of ideological consciousness formation. Such aversion, rather than being empowering, could be more likely to have the effect of providing endorsement for, and thus reinforce conservative, oppressive and reactionary modes of thought and practice. When it comes to intervening *in order to empower* it is Freire who provides a significant, if not totally satisfactory, example.

Freire, in his famous elucidation of the 'banking concept of education' (1972a, pp. 45–9), forcefully indicated that transferring or reproducing the teacher's knowledge in the pupil's mind is not necessarily empowering; just as the external imposition of meaning on situations is not necessarily emancipatory, nor is imposing liberating theory necessarily liberating. In fact, as Freire has compellingly demonstrated, such processes of 'depositing' might actually run counter to empowering, emancipating and liberating. The problem for Freire, however, and for those who have followed his lead, is what to replace the process of 'depositing' with. Freire's own notion of a shared teacher-pupil dialogical construction of meaning reads nicely and seductively, but along with Plato's demonstration in the *Meno*, it is not without its problems. Two of these should be noted here. First, there is the empirical matter that pupils, faced with a problem (or reduced to Socratic numbness) do not always, or even commonly, strive to seek out answers or to fill the void that critical questioning has created. And secondly, as Bowers (1984b, p. 96) and others have noted, it is questionable whether the sort of dialogue Freire advocates really does differ from imposition, or transcend and overcome the problem of cultural invasion and imperialism. Just as Socrates both set the problem for the slave boy and knew the right answer to begin with (for how else, other than by incalculable chance, could he have selected and structured his questions?) Freire too largely set the problems for his 'students', and also knew what would count as adequate answers in advance. In fact Freire's whole dialogical program becomes more than a little shaky once the point of achieving basic literacy is achieved (Walker, 1980). What do the pupils learn next, and who shall decide on content or judge when it is properly and correctly mastered? If a teacher is needed at all then this surely implies a limitation of some sort in the consciousness of the learner, as well as the desirability, judged from some point of view, of intervening (or engaging in some form of practice) with regard to that making good that limitation.

Serious problems become raised at this point, problems which, I suggest, can be accommodated and resolved by recasting the role of the teacher into a player of a three-phased sequence. If teachers sought first to expose contradictions in prevailing experience; secondly to assist others to act meaningfully and with power in reconstructing their experience; and thirdly to pass on skills and knowledge useful to all people in rational social reconstruction while at the same time actively recontextualizing the process of schooling itself — then the teaching act could become consistent with liberation and empowerment and the intervention involved would be potentially justifiable.

The construction of teaching as exposing and highlighting contradictions both within practice and between theory and practice, and then intervening to direct consciousness towards understanding and resolving these contradictions, is significant in three ways. First, it avoids essentialism. Second, it indicates that intervention can be liberating. And third, it moves significantly towards overcoming the problem noted earlier that radical critics made for themselves when they exposed cultural imperialism in liberal-essentialist curricula — namely how to substitute a curriculum for an essentialist one without at the same time leaning too far towards imperialism. Overall, it leads to the positive conclusion that intervention, which does not necessarily imply undue pressure or presenting content without reasons, can be liberating; while it does not in itself negate the possibility of constructing schooling as a site which develops skills for critical reflection and action as part of the struggle to overcome social inequity and create conditions conducive to genuine participatory democracy. The question that now becomes central is not whether knowledge and the curriculum can be empowering and emancipatory if they are, in practice, largely chosen and presented by teachers with powerful and privileged voices, but rather how to make them so.

Unfortunately, answers to this question have tended either to drift back towards a form of essentialism, where somewhere along the line a body of something suspiciously like essential content is identified, or else they suffer vagueness at the critical moment. Possibly the best and most fully articulated suggestions so far provided have been made by Patti Lather in a case which is by no means totally sympathetic, on important issues, to the one being built up here.

Lather (1986b), in attacking the problem of how to develop empowering approaches to generating knowledge, takes the standpoint outlined above that the real question facing those generating and transmitting knowledge is not how to be neutral or objective, but what to be committed to. True to her own beliefs, she then advocates a research program committed to the long-term, broad-based ideological struggle to transform structural inequalities, and argues that:

> theory adequate to the task of changing the world must be open-ended, non-dogmatic, informing, and grounded in the circum-stances of everyday life; and, moreover, it must be premised on a deep respect for the intellectual and political capacities of the dispossessed. (p. 262)

There are very strong shades of Freire and Walker here (as well as my own position, given my recognition of and respect for people's intel-lectual and political capacities, notwithstanding my account of the constitution of individuals as ideological subjects) as Lather advocates dialectical theory-building as an expression and elaboration of politi-cally progressive popular feelings, and, in the manner of those critics considered in chapter 2, deplores intellectuals imposing abstract frame-works on the complexity of lived experience. And the shades grow even stronger as she insists that building emancipatory social theory requires a ceaseless confrontation with, and respect for, the experience of people in their daily lives, to guard against theoretical imposition. Empowering theory and knowledge must, for Lather, both illuminate the lived experience of social groups and be illuminated by their strug-gles. It must be open-ended, dialogically reciprocal and grounded in respect for human capacity. But there is a catch to it all. Such theory and knowledge, Lather is at pains to stress, must also be profoundly sceptical of appearances and common sense, which, as Smith (1992) reminds us, is not an 'untheorized' view of the world but rather 'simply smuggles in one sort of theory rather than another' (p. 390). Thus Lather (1986b) advocates theory-building premised on the recognition 'that lived experience in an unequal society too often lacks an awareness of the need to struggle against privilege' (p. 262). Empowering critical inquiry in such a context must thus become a dialogic and mutually educative response to experience, but one which inspires and guides the dispossessed in the process of cultural transformation by focuss-ing 'on fundamental contradictions which help dispossessed people see how poorly their "ideologically frozen understandings" serve their interests' (*ibid*, p. 268).

Lather's position is clearly more sophisticated than much that I have been critical of. She shares the fairly common concern for starting with and respecting people's conceptions, capacities and desires, but she then voices the less common recognition or admission that these conceptions etc. could be inadequate and might possibly benefit by transformation and modification. Lather then openly charges the researcher, and by implication the teacher, with the very task of transformation and modification. She thus establishes a pedagogical context vibrating with the tension of teachers possessing a better-informed and more critical consciousness than their pupils (although not necessarily with regard to all possible contexts or about absolutely everything in their shared world) and who are committed to a political stance of enlightening and empowering without imposing.

This now brings us head on with the problem of intervention in teaching; as well as with the obligations of the teaching situation. And the simple reality is that one cannot be a teacher and neutrally lay out options or forever hold one's peace. To teach, which can include academics stating their cases in highly privileged legitimated contexts like journals and books, is to be interventionary. It is to state one's views, or at the weakest to place one's ideas 'on the agenda', and to do so from a position of privilege from which power and ascribed status cannot totally be removed.[2] Teachers who genuinely do not wish to intervene even this far, who do not wish to speak with a privileged voice, or who, paradoxically if not perversely, seek to persuade others not to do such things, might best stop teaching and publishing in order to avoid living out a contradiction. Those who are serious about teaching have the different problem of justifying their interventionary stance, along with the value of the substantive content they teach and the goals they seek through transmitting that content. And within that set those who wish to empower, liberate and transform need not seriously worry that their interventionary activities must necessarily place them in either a contradictory mode or else impose on them unbearable and unresolvable tensions. The key to escaping such modes and tensions hangs on the third point in the sequence indicated above, namely the knowledge transmitted in the teaching act along with the endeavour to reorient schooling itself.

Teachers and the Reorientation of Schooling

I indicated in the previous section that much of what I am proposing revolves around teachers transmitting skills and knowledge which will be useful to all people in the task of rational social reconstruction. To this point, however, little detail has been given concerning the substantive content of the curriculum which it would be the teacher's responsibility to guard, foster and transmit (and about which, it will be suggested, teachers ought have reflexive awareness concerning its interrelationship with power and consciousness-formation). In this section I want to make good a portion of that deficiency. I shall do this, perhaps surprisingly, by arguing for the retention of a considerable part of the traditional liberal curriculum. I shall also argue, however, for significantly broadening and recontextualizing that curriculum in order to include additional voices and to serve a greater set of interests.

Curricula, as noted above, are finite packages selected from the infinite realm of knowledge for the alleged purpose of developing certain selected human values, competencies and skills, themselves drawn from an infinite pool, which are deemed valuable by people and groups privileged to make such decisions. The idealist tradition tends to distinguish between physical and mental skills, and to recognize only the latter, and then even only some of the latter, to be really educative. A materialist approach to human development and education would avoid dualisms such as the distinction between the mental and the physical, just as it would avoid essentialism. This does not (as some would claim) necessarily lead to relativism and/or entail that all knowledge and skills should be regarded as important or valuable, let alone equally important or valuable, or important or valuable in every social instance. What, from a materialist context, makes knowledge and skills valued, and thus worthy of being fostered and promoted, are (again) not metaphysical and/or essentialist considerations, but rather specific considerations of social and political utility, along with the service of particular interests and needs of particular social formations. Literary criticism, for instance, has no essential intrinsic worth: it may be extremely valuable in some sociohistoric contexts and absurdly useless in others. But while materialism does not rely on essentialist and/or metaphysical criteria to determine what is valuable or worthwhile, it also does not deny or preclude certain things from appearing more or less constantly throughout history as they are continually evaluated, not as being worthwhile in themselves or as vitally related to 'human nature' or abstractions such as improvement of 'the human condition' or 'the quality of life', but rather as being centrally related to the existence and development of humans as historical and social beings. There are elements of the liberal curriculum that can be seen and defended in precisely this way.

A fairly obvious stumbling block to mounting such a defence, however, is the common recognition that things which may have been continually evaluated as being worthwhile to human social and historical development in general have not always, or even commonly, been employed or directed to such ends. Rather, it is undoubtedly the case that certain human capacities, capabilities, ways of thinking, forms of enquiry and bodies of knowledge have been utilized and legitimated in past and present societies for securing, preserving and perpetuating ruling rather than general interests. For instance, that which has been traditionally legitimated as great literature has tended to glorify and promote particular ruling values and life-styles, while much recorded and well-regarded history is clearly class-biased, racist, sexist, and paints a picture of the past and of human progress which clearly serves particular ruling interests. But past usage does not necessarily mean that certain broad bodies of knowledge and methodology which have (and do) serve ruling interests might not be important to know, do, practice, preserve and pass on if, *recontextualized*, they might also serve the interests of all humanity and constitute an important and relevant means for engaging with practical and theoretical problems pertinent to the survival and rational reconstruction of any particular social or-ganization. The fact that forms and aspects of history, literature, science and mathematics have been used throughout history as a means of oppression provides no argument against teaching and studying litera-ture, history, etc. themselves, and it certainly does not establish that history, literature, science and mathematics are necessarily enemies of the oppressed. Rather, properly understood and recontextualized they can provide some of the tools for and be part of the driving force of social reconstruction seeking equity, autonomy, genuine democratic participation and the continued manifestation and exercise of worthwhile human qualities, capacities and endeavours.

Social reconstruction, or constructing the future, may thus require not that we reject the programatic knowledge and methodologies so far built up in our hard-won heritage (some of which is continually rep-resented in the liberal curriculum) but rather that we place this content, justify it where possible on non-essentialist criteria, significantly broaden its base by including previously and presently excluded voices, and thus continually refine and further a more fully inclusive heritage. The programmatic content, along with the overt and officially stated aims and objectives of the liberal curriculum, are in fact largely well suited to fostering human excellences, moral understanding and rational social development. The problem that has arisen historically and politically in basing schooling for all, and thus for oppressed groups, on such a curriculum lies more in the areas of orientation and accessibility.

In chapter 1 I outlined the manner in which liberal ideals and egalitarian motives were rationalized in the provision of universal com-pulsory schooling, and how concerns were then raised that such schooling, through having to cater for and direct resources to all, might bring about a lowering of standards and offerings for the most able. What were lost here were the original motives and concerns for bringing the best of quality and opportunity to all. Perhaps ironically, those are the concerns that have now to be revived if we are to build a world not where cobblers cobble while the wise rule for them, but one in which all can participate autonomously in a free and democratic context.

This, as I have just indicated, does not require that we throw out the content of the liberal curriculum, almost as a matter of principle or as some form of revenge for history. Rather, that content might better be reoriented in context, enlarged in scope and changed in detail towards deliberately presenting a significantly modified message. I do not want to get bogged down here in matters of substantive detail, which can be better debated elsewhere, but in this context teachers (especially of the sort I am advocating) might enlarge the scope of, say, literary studies by recognizing that literature may have reached pinnacles with Shakespeare and Keats but it did not end there, and so both include voices such as those of Toni Morrison and Derek Walcott and at the same time justify and defend such inclusions. And as for accessibility, both the policy underlying the provision of schooling and the practice of schooling itself have to be modified such that schools really do become an acceptable and legitimate place and means of learning for the working class and other oppressed and minority groups. These are the groups who actually have to get more of schooling and get more out of schooling; but also be offered their schooling in a form which includes and attends to their voices, which is more suited to their needs and which is better placed to engage in and promote rational social reconstruction.

The point of the reorientation is central. The aim is not to provide more inclusive and recontextualized liberal studies so that those suffering oppression might individually have the chance to do better under the existing economic and social system (and perhaps themselves become oppressors); but rather so that, both given a voice and armed with a greater range of the recorded manifestations of historical human achievement, all people might become better informed, more rounded, more receptive and more capable of understanding human existence, in order to become better placed to exercise their capacities to control the present and construct the future. Undertaking such an enterprise would require, as Matthew Arnold (1963) put it, 'turning a stream of fresh and free thought' upon our stock notions and habits' (p. 6), or (as Arnold might not have put it) seeing the world from a wider perspective than the viewpoints dictated by the needs of a ruling class, or by 'working class culture' or even by the particular concerns of any specific interest group. The ultimate move envisaged is a dramatic one towards a real liberating education; one which liberates the oppressed from their intellectual and political contexts simultaneously.

Two final things ought to be noted. First, the content referred to above in terms of its links and parallels with the broad outlines of the traditional liberal curriculum would not by any means represent the whole of the content of schooling. Schooling recontextualized in the manner indicated above would promote vocational and instrumental content as well; but this would get neither the prominent place many economic rationalists are now advocating, nor would it be endowed with the lesser status idealism tends to bestow or be regarded as a subsidiary nuisance factor getting in the way of the school's real work. Secondly, it is hardly being suggested that schooling would necessarily start with some historically 'agreed-on' body of 'worthwhile knowledge', with specifically 'Western knowledge', or that the very same manifestations of recorded human endeavour would be fostered and promoted in all social or physical contexts. Under what is being proposed here the periodic table of the elements is not about to be foisted on tribal dwellers in the Amazon basin. What knowledge might be promoted will be considered further in the concluding chapter.

Conclusion

To teach is always to intervene to some extent, even if only by expressing a powerful voice in setting an agenda. This is an outcome even the most progressive of child-centred educationists, such as A.S.Neill, could not circumvent. The issue at the school level, I would think, is not to defer from or diminish teacher intervention in the lives of the young. Nor is it to look beyond teachers for setting the curriculum agenda, either by placing this in the province of government or by having it negotiated with the pupils through intercultural articulation. It is, rather, to produce knowledgeable teachers, committed to improving historical-human conditions, who can provide informed reasoned justification for both their stance and for the substantive content they guard, further and profess; who are committed to a more inclusive reorientation of schooling and its content; and who in turn could be that section of the citizenry whose opinions on schooling and curriculum, and even on the good, should justly be privileged over others.

How to produce the teachers I am speaking of, what qualities they should bear, and why I am placing a burden as great as promoting social reconstruction on teachers rather than other groups in society, will be discussed in the next chapter.

Notes

1 This recognition moves significantly towards overcoming some elementary errors I made in *Education and Knowledge* (1979), some of which have been noted above and for most of which I have been justly and soundly criticized.
2 A large literature, ranging from Saussure's pioneering work early in this century through to the influential recent production of Bourdieu and Foucault, indicates power to be an integral part of the very language, and thus the body of discourse, generated from particular sources.

Chapter 7

Teachers as Intellectual Vanguard

Introduction

Teaching, regardless of how a few of the more cynical might see the job, entails an intellectual concern with the transmission and advancement of knowledge, a moral concern for human betterment, and a more general concern to combat not just ignorance but also the commonplace. This is not to say, of course, that every single teacher embraces such concerns, that many others outside of teaching may not also hold them, or that individual persons may not have their own idiosyncratic reasons for becoming teachers. But outside the realm of the idiosyncratic we might seriously question why people would commit their working life to an endeavour centred on forming new generations if they did not have some particular interest in transmitting knowledge and contributing to a process of social and historical advancement.

In this chapter I want to set a context which can take up some of the issues raised in earlier chapters and which can also encompass and develop the notion of the teacher as a person bearing expertise in some knowledge area who is concerned both with transmitting and sharing that knowledge and promoting human betterment. A profitable way of filling that out can be approached through considering and developing the well-worked notion of the teacher-as-intellectual.

The Teacher-as-Intellectual

The idea of the teacher-as-intellectual is hardly new, but it has recently become fashionable in some quarters, resulting in a large body of literature on that issue having been built up in the last decade.[1] Within that literature one of the more interesting analyses has been that of Aronowitz and Giroux (1985, pp. 23–45), who identify four readily recognizable types of intellectuals within the educative milieu. First there are 'accommodating intellectuals', who stand firmly within ideological postures and sets of material practices that support the dominant society and its ruling groups. Next come 'critical intellectuals', who are ideologically alternative to existing institutions and modes of thought, but who adopt a self-consciously apolitical posture, and attempt to define their relationship to the rest of society as free-floating. 'Hegemonic intellectuals' self-consciously provide forms of moral and intellectual leadership for dominant groups and classes. And finally there are 'transformative intellectuals', who advance emancipatory traditions and cultures. It is the transformative intellectual that Aronowitz and Giroux look to in terms of desirable pedagogy and social change.

Transformative intellectuals, as Aronowitz and Giroux characterize them, occupy contradictory, paradoxical and tension-filled roles within formal educational institutions. They earn their living within those institutions that are fundamental in producing and legitimating the dominant culture and social practices, but in doing so they offer alternative discourse and critical social practices which are often at odds with the role of the very institution they work in and the social practices which support it. Like all teachers at all levels they are pressured, subtly and otherwise, to engage with the issues, and follow the forms of research, discourse and social practices legitimated by the dominant culture, but to be 'transformative' they must struggle against being incorporated by the very system which employs them, and which tends to disproportionately reward employees who are willing to remove critical scholarship and/or political commitment from their teaching. Further, as Aronowitz and Giroux put it, they:

> must take active responsibility for raising serious questions about what they teach, how they are to teach it, and what the larger goals are for which they are striving. This means that they must take a responsible role in shaping the purposes and conditions of schooling. (*ibid*, p. 31)

This is a valuable formulation worthy of careful consideration and support. In the final analysis, however, it is just a little too simplistic. In places it comes dangerously close to Karl Mannheim's rather naive stance (1966, pp. 136–46) of postulating a class of detached disinterested intelligensia operating within society, and by veering in that direction it glosses over the very point I have been at some pains to stress and keep in the limelight of this developing discussion: namely that (transformative) intellectuals are themselves ideological subjects who must somehow both recognize and partly 'transcend' their own structural ideological consciousness-formation. To miss this point, or to gloss over it, is to miss the real complexity of the situation. It is also to miss the possibility of a solution.

A better direction to turn to is that taken by Gramsci (1976, pp. 3–23). Gramsci argues that all people, being centres of consciousness, are intellectuals in that sense, but only some people choose, or are properly placed to function as intellectuals in society. These intellectuals, he argues further, undertake 'diverse and disparate activities' and are characterized not by the intrinsic nature of their intellectual pursuits but rather by the social role they perform and the place their intellectual activities have 'within the general complex of social relations'. In referring to intellectuals, then, Gramsci is referring to a category of people who are identifiable and categorizable only in the context of their performance of a social function. They are not, however, an independent and autonomous group. Central to Gramsci's conception of intellectuals is their necessary connection with either an established or an emerging social group (more exactly, with a socioeconomic class in classical Marxist terms). Every social group of this type, Gramsci argues, 'creates together with itself, organically, one or more strata of intellectuals which give it homogeneity and an awareness of its own function not only in the economic but also in the social and political fields' (*ibid*, p. 5).

These intellectuals are not of a single sort. On the one hand there are 'traditional' intellectuals. They are products of past history who, mainly because of their long historical continuity, believe themselves to be independent of the prevailing dominant socioeconomic group and thus see themselves as performing a pure intellectual function rather than a political or ideological function. Their relationship and service to particular class relations and interests is largely concealed both to themselves and to society. Gramsci points to ecclesiastics for an example; a particular sub-group of academics would serve just as well. On the other hand there are 'organic' intellectuals which every new class creates in and alongside itself to perform the social function of developing the critical self-consciousness of the historical moment of the emergence of that class. It is their distinguishable social function to challenge and overcome existing traditional intellectuals, to establish and refine systematic theoretic frameworks, to seek precision and offer direction for political activity, to make coherent 'the principles and the problems raised by the masses in their practical activity' (*ibid*, p. 330) and to organize and lead an emerging age by concretely grounding and elaborating the theoretical aspect of its developing praxis. (Over a long historical period they may become traditional intellectuals to be confronted by the next emergence of organic intellectuals.)

Three points regarding these organic intellectuals should be stressed. First, they belong to, are connected with and come from within the emerging class, and their experience is, and remains, part of the emergence of the class and the historical movement whose theoretic and political position they define and refine. Their background and experience 'lies within' the ideological representation and social construction of that class, while their acquired reflexive awareness provides the opportunity for evaluating that experience from a broader perspective. The theory they bear is thus illuminated by, and itself further illuminates, the experience and struggles of that emerging class.

Secondly, they are identifiable not specifically by their 'theory' (which may be sophisticated but need hardly be perfect: they can be learners as well as teachers) but by their actual function, along with their practical commitment, in leading and directing the political history of the class they organically belong to. Their function and practice ought thus be anything but imposing abstract frameworks on experience.

Thirdly, by their very nature and location they are placed in a relationship of challenge to existing social relations.

These points, taken together, particularly distinguish organic intellectuals as people who could be expected to be relatively well placed to have some awareness and recognition of their own initial constitution as ideological subjects, and to use that recognition as a basis for actively promoting awareness not only that factors militate against people coming to evaluate and construct knowledge and understanding of their world, but also that people can be helped in this regard by others who are more fully and/or better informed and/or more opportunely placed. If this is the case then we might justifiably promote producing teachers who fit the Gramscian model of organic intellectuals, and then endorse and echo Gramsci's call to these intellectuals to assist people to become increasingly conscious of their own actions and situation in the world.

Teachers are particularly well placed with regard to performing this function on at least four counts. First, they are expert bearers of knowledge, the nature and substance of which I have alluded to in the previous chapter and will consider again in the following one. What needs to be added here is the recognition that, unlike most other expertly informed interest groups, teachers are professionally committed to transmitting and sharing their knowledge. While certain other knowledgeable professions tend to guard and/or mystify their specialized knowledge, teachers work themselves to a frazzle in an attempt to share theirs around as widely as possible, and end up rewarding and praising those pupils who learn and assimilate what has been offered.

Secondly, teachers differ from virtually all the other interest groups in society who are similarly undertaking the endeavour of forming consciousness, including those groups with moral concerns such as the churches and those with intellectual concerns, such as some sections of industry, in that teachers are engaging in both a non-sectarian and a non-commercial enterprise. Although 'payment by results' was once part of the industrial conditions of teaching in some places and has reemerged in certain current market-oriented proposals as a supposed means of making teaching more accountable and 'efficient', there is at present generally no monetary profit for teachers to make in success-fully plying their wares. There are also no converts to sectarian causes to be won. Teachers, virtually uniquely, engage in the process of forming consciousness for the potential benefit of their pupils, and for society and humanity as a whole; but not (although the weekly pay packet is an important and relevant factor) for the benefit of themselves or of any specific commercial or sectarian interest. Their commitment is to the emerging generation and the future.

Thirdly, teachers, unlike say company lawyers or advertising agents, are not objectively committed to, or dependent on, the social relations of capitalism for their survival, either as an occupational group or as agents in the process of social change. They will be as much needed in a society reconstructed along genuine democratic and non-exploita-tive principles and practices as they are now (as will be the liberating knowledge they guard, profess and further); and so, although there might be individual casualties, teachers are in a position where they actually can work as a coherent interest group seeking and promoting social reconstruction without the danger of, in doing so, bringing about their own eventual collective demise. Although, as is the case with all skilled professionals under capitalism, teachers are candidates for proletarianization, they are also quite well placed politically to work against the very conditions which generate and feed the prole-tarianization process in the first place.

Finally, if not exhaustively, teachers have history on their side in that, presently, even though some minority groups are not well rep-resented among them, their numbers overwhelmingly come from emerging groups within society. Teaching draws heavily from the working class and from women, such that the teaching force as pres-ently constituted has been created in and alongside, and is organic to, what could be the historical emergence of significant social, political and interest groups. Teachers are particularly well placed to perform the social function of developing the critical self-consciousness of that historical movement.

Teaching and Professional Knowledge

It is difficult to imagine anyone arguing that teachers ought not have expert knowledge of the substantive content of the subject area which they teach. An issue that has reemerged recently, however, (it had some support towards the end of the nineteenth century) is that some (for example, Lawlor, 1990) are proposing that this expertise in content knowledge is just about all the professional knowledge teachers need to have. On the one hand it is being suggested that educational theory and knowledge in related areas such as sociology of education and philosophy of education is not only unnecessary for classroom teachers, but also that it may be positively harmful for them in that it might make them critical of, rather than unquestioningly proficient in, the work that they do. On the other hand it is also being suggested that teaching, unlike (say) law and medicine, is a fairly low-skilled business which just about anyone could do and which hardly requires years of pre-service professional education. From this it is taken as following that once teachers have gained their expertise in content knowledge the best thing to do would be to put them in schools where they can pick up the 'teaching tips' they need in the best of all possible places, namely on the job. Thus we have at least one rationale for current proposals to move away from tertiary-based initial teacher education to school-based continuing teacher training, as well as for growing practices to employ untrained (and unregistered) people as teachers on the basis of their content-knowledge and presumably their suitable personal credentials.[2] Such proposals, in their best possible light, can be seen as shifting a necessary concentration on to the practical aspects of teaching, and in this regard a massive literature (a virtual education sub-industry) has been generated focussing first on the practicum, and now in response to moves towards devolution, on day-to-day as well as larger issues concerning local management of schooling. In a less-flattering if more realistic light these proposals can be recognized as part of a larger contemporary move to hasten and intensify the proletarianization of teachers through deprofessionalization (discrediting the notion of the critical practitioner) and deskilling (reducing teaching to instrumental classroom actions).

There are, I believe, good and worthwhile reasons for moving in very much the opposite direction. The proposals outlined above have the clear merit of at least recognizing the necessity and worth of teachers' content knowledge, along with the undoubted value of on-the-job experience, and they may (although history offers a warning with regard to this) lead to the production of efficient classroom functionaries. The point, however, is that teaching is far more than engaging in instructional activities in classrooms from 9.00 in the morning to 3.00 or 4.00 in the afternoon, five days a week. Teaching, as indicated at the very beginning of this chapter, entails a moral dimension concerned with, and related to, human betterment. Teachers, whether they wish it or not, in performing their classroom instructional activities at the same time affect the development of each individual child as a person. Teachers also, again whether they wish it or not, engage in, globally, the production of the future citizens of society and in some part construct that future society itself along lines considered desirable from some particular point of view.

Recognized in this sort of light teaching is revealed as a highly responsible, deeply influential social and historical activity, and there is surely justification in suggesting that it be performed by highly educated, socially and professionally responsible people. Deskilling teachers *qua* teachers through narrowing and/or restricting their practical activities in the classroom and directing more of their energies and efforts into management, and deprofessionalizing and disempowering teachers by reducing or removing their critical input with regard to educational policy and practice, would lessen teaching's effect in this regard. Such practices may, in all likelihood, serve a larger-scale purpose of producing greater compliance and less critical awareness among the emerging generation of citizens, which may have some short-term effect in helping to bed down, with minimal social disruption, criticism or expression of discontent, microeconomic changes and the attendant modified social relations designed to assist the current internationalization of capital accumulation. And this in turn might satisfy the aspirations and ideals of market-oriented pragmatists and economic rationalists, not to mention, of course, capitalists and those well served by the capitalist mode of production; but it does otherwise seem to represent a potentially fearful narrowing of historical possibilities and to entail enormous wastage of, and disregard for, human potential. This is especially so for those among the poor, the oppressed and the disadvantaged who will not be well served by current micro-economic restructuring designed to secure, first and foremost, conditions conducive to the accumulation of capital. Reskilling and reprofessionalizing teachers, on the other hand, through providing them with more refined teaching skills, with more advanced content knowledge, with a high level of reflexive knowledge and awareness, and then giving them greatly increased power over educational policy, is more likely to result in a teaching force that would not be easily content with such ends or with such wastage of potential; and which would also be better placed to assist with the production of, and help lead, a knowledgeable critical citizenry capable of acting autonomously in the construction of its own desired future.

I have already noted teaching's relationship with a concern for human betterment. For the teacher-as-intellectual that concern could usefully be extended to commitment; not to the commonly proposed neutralist position, but rather commitment to social reconstruction on rational and genuine democratic lines. As I have indicated earlier, once it is recognized that there is no neutral education we need no longer apologize for an open commitment to using education to criticize and change the status quo. Teaching and schooling practices that challenge the status quo in order to produce a social order in which people can live autonomous lives and participate in the democratic exercise and control of political power, are as objective as any, and I would think more justifiable than most. However, in the case of teachers deliberately promoting such a position the commitment required, as with the entire interventionary teaching act, should be informed, justified and rational.

There is good reason to suggest that teachers would be better placed to assist in producing a critical citizenry, and to justify their actions on a rational basis, if they themselves were practised in rationality and critical scholarship. To these ends they would be benefited by being led beyond their expertise in substantive curriculum areas and, rather than being 'detheorized', were introduced to those fields of theoretic enquiry and practical and theoretic methodologies which developed 'critical self-consciousness' and enabled them to understand theory, apply theory and be soundly critical of theory and practices, including their own. They would be well served by engaging with content and methodologies which enabled them to formulate and elaborate complex theoretical stances, which enabled them to articulate and be critical of policy, and especially which developed in them an awareness of the way both knowledge itself, as well as 'having' that knowledge, interacts with power, discourse and the formation of consciousness. This represents a highly significant broadening of the knowledge base commonly exposed and explored in teacher education programs (and, *inter alia*, a call for broadening and rigorously extending such programs) in order to produce not just the reflective teacher but rather *reflexive teachers*. Armed with and informed by such knowledge these reflexive teachers would not automatically escape their initial constitution as ideological subjects, nor is it being suggested that they would come to totally transcend such constitution. But it is reasonable to suggest that they might be better placed to *understand* it; that is, to recognize how structures impact on consciousness to produce ideological subjects, and then to use this recognition as an early and continuing step in leading and developing the consciousness of their pupils. If such teachers also recognized how discourse embodies socially constructed classifications and categorizations of the world, and how their professional discourse has presently been appropriated (largely by economic rationalism), they might also become better placed to collectively regain control of that discourse in order (eventually) that they themselves might set the educational agenda. They might also then, with justified conviction, promote and direct an agenda set towards the end of producing the autonomous, informed, political, moral and cultural agents that collectively constitute a civilized democratic society.

Conclusion

What has been said in this and the preceding chapter about a liberal (as in liberating) curriculum, recontextualizing schooling itself, and the teacher-as-intellectual is, in something of a roundabout way, to accept the major criticisms rather than repeat the central error of crude reproduction theory. It is to recognize that social reproduction is an active and contested business. But it is also to accept that people may need, or at the least might benefit from, informed assistance and leadership in what Willis (1977) called 'the challenge of the day to day' (p. 186). And with the 'challenge of the day to day' now on the agenda this becomes an appropriate time to consider particular details relating to those teachers who would undertake the (transformative) challenge of enlightening and empowering pupils, and reorienting schools, toward rationally constructing future social conditions which promoted enlightened democratic participation of the citizenry. It is necessary, at least, to indicate why teachers should choose and determine the knowledge that shall make up the curriculum, and why I am placing so large a part of the task of social reconstruction on teachers in the first place.

Notes

1   See, for instance, Smyth (1987a), and especially the comprehensive bibliography included.

2   It is not uncommon today to find countries in which veterinary surgeons have to be rigorously trained, and registered, but no such requirements are made regarding teachers. People in such places can be reassured that their cat's worming is being administered by a qualified registered person but may have no such assurance regarding their children's education.

Chapter 8

Conclusion

Introduction

In concluding this overall essay I shall attempt to put three final pieces in place by indicating why it should be teachers who largely determine what knowledge shall make up the curriculum; why I am placing so large a part of the burden for social reconstruction on teachers in the first place; and what teachers might reasonably be expected to achieve in the current and foreseeable circumstances.

Why Teachers Should Control Curricula

My argument for teacher control of the curriculum (and even further, control of the purposes and goals of schooling itself) begins with the recognition that every social formation has its own historical construction of what knowledge and which human capacities are desirable and are thus to be fostered and developed, and centres on the deliberate and long emphasis on the 'ideological subject' provided in chapter 4. The position taken there unashamedly, and perhaps unpopularly, proposes that all people's knowledge and understanding of all things is not equal or equally valid. It does not, however, malign or ignore individuals' intellectual and political capacities, nor does it propose that some people are smarter than others, or that some people are naturally dumb or function as zombies either through choice or structural pressure. Rather, it argues that consciousness is larg y sociohistorically determined; that within sociohistoric moments some agencies or apparatuses are better placed to determine what knowledge and values are to be promoted; that people do not come by their knowledge and values freely or naturally but rather in a contested yet patently unequal if dynamic power situation; and that within sociohistoric moments some people become better placed to be critical and in a sense 'transcend' the dominant forms and substance of consciousness and value-formation. Given all of that, what I am seeking is teachers, as a sub-set rather than the totality of people who have become better placed to be critical, being more prominently situated with regard to determining the knowledge and values to be legitimated and promoted within societies.

This is not to deny, of course, that there may be much knowledge and many questions and problems that people will, unaided, come to learn, answer and solve very adequately in their lives. But it is also to recognize that there are ways of seeing things and contextualizing issues and problems that are unlikely to be just stumbled on or picked up as part of 'common sense', and which have to be 'promoted' if they are to become and continue to constitute part of the social/intellectual environment. The state's apparatuses, including and along with the media, are extremely powerful and have little compunction in promoting ideas and values which serve the ruling interests of the state, or in delegitimating conceptualizations and practices which work against the perceived interests of the state; and given this it is hardly perverse to recommend intellectuals in society undertaking the same form of promotion but for different ends. On the other hand, commercial interests in society similarly have little compunction in promoting things which tend towards the mediocre and the banal, such as much of today's ephemeral 'pop' music, TV 'soaps' and game shows, pulp paperbacks and 'action' movies and videos, along with attendant franchised and syndicated products like T-shirts and posters that, having been bought, generate additional profit and further promote their source. In that context it is similarly not perverse, while not deriding all popular art and literature, and while recognizing that even the utterly banal and ephemeral has a place in individual and social development and experience, to recommend that intellectuals undertake a similar but non-commercial form of promotion of art, music, literature and movies of a distinctly different quality, along with science, mathematics, history, philosophy, sociology and so on. Literary and artistic merit, like complex scientific, mathematical, social and political theory, is commonly not intrinsically or demonstratively noticeable to most children learning to conceptualize the world and construct their experience in it, and in the face of the commercial promotion of ephemeral mediocrity it could well have a few champions and promoters of its own. This, then, is simply to put the case for the place and worth of schools and intellectuals. It is not to elevate schooling *qua* schooling to some privileged essentialist or idealist form, nor is it to suggest that schooling constitutes, or ought constitute, the whole of worthwhile experience. Rather it is merely to recognize that schooling, like all the apparatuses and manifestations previously mentioned, not only has a place in social-intellectual development but also that it is a special place for fostering and promoting a particular type of consciousness and awareness.

Much the same holds for intellectuals. They are not the only source of knowledge and values within a society, but they do have a place, and as I have been suggesting for some time now teachers-as-intellectuals would be well placed, on a number of grounds, to undertake the sort of promotion I have just referred to, as well as to transmit and advance knowledge suitable to, and capable of, empowering people to become critically aware of the world and to function as autonomous citizens within a democratic society.

Teachers are, as has been commonly noted, 'guardians of legitimate knowledge and gate-keepers for advancement' (Connell *et al*, 1982, p. 196). They have, through their own schooling and pre-service teacher-education programs, been more widely and deeply exposed to knowledge sources than has the broad base of society in general, and they are, at the least, bearers of advanced levels of the content they are to teach. (Their additional schooling could, on its own, serve to con-stitute them more deeply and fully as ideological subjects: thus my continual championing of teachers undertaking the sort of studies which can place their expert content in its wider social, cultural and historical setting and which might give teachers a reflexive awareness of their own role with regard to the transmission of knowledge). In addition to this, teachers (virtually uniquely) have expert knowledge in how to convey and transmit content. This is highly complex and advanced knowledge, which ought neither be underestimated nor trivialized. There may be many in society who know far more about certain areas of content than most teachers do, but unlike such people in general, and notwithstanding the few charismatic 'born teachers' around, teachers are also specialized experts in transmitting content and structuring ex-periences that facilitate learning. And finally, as noted earlier, teachers are 'special' bearers of knowledge in that they are committed in principle and bound in practice to sharing their knowledge and to fostering and promoting human betterment through this process. It might be added here that in all these respects teachers differ markedly from both the elected representatives and the public service bureaucrats who together constitute the process of government.

This is hardly to suggest, however, that teachers know best about all things, or that they have had the experiences which consistently give them a privileged place in understanding people's needs and perceptions of the world, let alone in actually understanding the world itself as seen from particular experiential viewpoints. James Baldwin is alleged to have said that you have to be black, gay and poor to know what it means to be black, gay and poor; and this sort of expression certainly does encapsulate a popular sentiment. It is very much the sentiment that prompted those radical critics cited earlier to advocate refraining from intervening in the lives of others on the grounds that outsiders could not possibly know what other people's real perceptions, feelings and needs were, and so were likely to act in the manner of missionaries imposing meanings on experience.

There is a lot in this, but not quite as much as is often made out. If it is the case that one has to be black, gay and poor to understand what it means to be black, gay and poor, which in terms of educational policy strongly suggests that you have to be these things in order to teach and to formulate policy regarding those who are black, gay and poor, then the sentiment or principle becomes self-defeating on two grounds. On the one hand, unless highly generalized variables are inserted (and the more general they are the less bite the principle has) it could disqualify virtually everybody from teaching anybody else. And on the other hand, where the principle does or might permit teaching to take place it could very easily restrict and limit the potential educative exchange within the confines of otherwise established ghettos. It might thus engender sympathetic teaching and learning, as blacks teach blacks, gays teach gays, women teach women and so on, but this is hardly the whole of the recipe required for expanding the knowledge and horizons of those being taught (and those teaching). This particular point also raises what could be called 'Raskolnikoff's problem'. Dostoyevsky's character believed he had to commit the crime of murder in order to really know how a murderer felt. This may ultimately be so, but it is a position so extreme as to impose an almost ludicrous element onto the criteria for knowledge and experience. If we really have to be black, gay and have been born poor or give up all our wealth in order to really know how blacks, gays and the poor experience the world, or at least to teach them adequately, then effective teaching of virtually anybody, anywhere, is rendered very very difficult and unlikely.

There is, of course, something far more obviously imperialistic, yet potentially defeating, in the vision of a white upper class straight male coming directly from an insulated privileged social upbringing and a university education, carrying a basket of 'the best that has been thought and said in the world' (by white upper class males, as it almost always turns out), and offering this to poor oppressed people of colour for their liberation and salvation. The temptation to go for an alternative like intercultural articulation here is understandable.

Yielding to that temptation, however, makes one vulnerable to accepting too easily and uncritically, and possibly even appropriating, what Lather called 'ideologically frozen understandings'. A better alternative is to steer well between surrender and appropriation: to carry one's own sociocultural and intellectual baggage (as one must) and at the same time to attempt as far as possible to understand what it means to be the other when coming to the educational exchange (which, again, is anything but imposing the periodic table of the elements on Amazonians who may have no need for it). To act in this way is to further take on the form and role of Gramsci's organic intellectuals, who function in society in such a way that every teacher is a pupil and every pupil is a teacher (Gramsci, 1976, p. 350). It is also to substitute the real possibility of reflexive teaching for the impossibility of shared replication or reconstitution of the life experience of the educand, as well as to make possible, through reflexive studies, genuine recognition of the limitations of both learning partners in the educative exchange. It demands, of course, a high level of sensitive intellectual development on the part of the teacher.

Eventually it comes down to what best can be done in a real finite limited world where someone has to take responsibility for 'shaping the purposes and conditions of schooling', and where in fact 'someone' already quite deliberately does determine curricula on political grounds. This responsibility can hardly be borne, let alone realized effectively, by 'the citizenry as a whole', and 'intercultural articulation' is also not a sufficiently suitable basis for such an endeavour. This leaves us, realistically, with expert educationists and the government. Of these the teacher-as-intellectual, being the end product of an extensive occupation-specific as well as a rigorous general education program, appears better suited for the task than members of the government who have their own political agenda to follow and who are also less specifically selected and educated. Although a choice between representatives of government and intellectuals who are educational experts with regard to who should formulate educational policy, construct school curricula and determine notions of the good life should be minimally difficult to make, perhaps any last lingering doubts might be dispelled by attending to Chomsky's observation (1971) that 'Intellectuals are in a position to expose the lies of governments . . .' (p. 256).

Having teachers formulate educational policy, construct school curricula and determine notions of the good life requires, among other things, that teachers have greater control over their conditions of work. I shall examine that possibility in a later section.

Teachers as Vanguard in Social Reconstruction

It might appear from what I have said in the previous section that I have done nothing more than come full circle back to Plato and the others I have quoted like Arnold, Leavis and Peters, who suggested that a minority carries the standards for human existence and advancement, and who (apart from Peters) advocated that this minority should be set up as guardians of culture and intervene on humanity's behalf.

In reality it is a little more complex than that. With regard to a minority bearing the best of knowledge and values Plato and his followers were, in one sense, right. There is always a minority of highly advanced specialists at what is commonly referred to as the 'cutting edge' of bodies of knowledge and enquiry, and it almost always is the case that this minority does have to promote its knowledge or 'intervene' in order that excellences are pursued, errors corrected and the commonplace countered. That much is not necessarily elitism; and it need not generate conflict with democratic purposes. Where the Platonic and idealist tradition has gone wrong is in its accounts of how and why such a situation has come about, along with certain unwarranted generalizations following from those accounts. This is especially so in the way that tradition makes recourse to human nature as a causal and explanatory factor; in its alleged revelation of the worthwhile through essentialism and its identification of so much of the worthwhile with ruling class values; in its related dismissal of much other knowledge and many other voices; in its failure to understand how minorities holding and perpetuating particular knowledge (and values) are themselves products and manifestations of the divisions that characterize class societies; and in its often stated assumptions that experts in one or some areas of knowledge almost automatically become experts in issues of social development and bearers of particularly fine and desirable values. But recognizing those errors, and taking care not to repeat them, does not necessarily deny or rule out of court the possibility of teachers, as an enlightened minority of commercially-disinterested guardians and gate-keepers of knowledge and values in the present historical conjuncture, restructuring and reorienting the very material they bear and guard for the end of contributing towards the construction of a truly just and universally enlightened democratic society. As Lankshear (1987) has suggested the subtlety of the demand is to place one's skills in the service of the subordinated while at the same time consciously opting out of attendant social relations of ascribed status (p. 240). I do not think, as I have previously indicated, that teachers can totally avoid ascribed status or adopting some form of privileged position regarding power relations, but at least making the attempt, as well as operating within the sort of context where every teacher is a pupil and every pupil is a teacher, would move significantly towards dissolving the 'problem' of teachers intervening in the lives of their charges for the purpose of making them free, critical and autonomous agents.

A major lingering problem here is that it has been largely those working within the idealist tradition who have promoted the potentially liberating aspects of intervention; while those adopting radical perspectives have tended, with insufficiently critical ease, to categorize and identify deliberate teacher-intervention as imperialist and oppressive. This historical failure, by those standing outside the idealist tradition, to recognize or accept the potentially liberating nature of intervention is both damaging and counterproductive in a world where ideological apparatuses work with extreme sophistication in forming consciousness (this includes those state apparatuses which determine school curricula), and in which commercial interests are able to exert similarly enormous influence over thought, values and consciousness. In a sociohistoric context in which people simply do not come naturally to what is worthwhile, nor easily, regardless of their capacities and ability, choose rationally and autonomously, let alone freely, among options, teachers are well placed and have good reason to be directly involved with pupils' futures and social reconstruction. Teachers deliberately form consciousness, and schools are sites for the formal undertaking of that project. As I indicated earlier schooling is not the whole of experience and it is certainly not the whole of worthwhile experience, and teachers in no way have a monopoly on knowledge, wisdom and the worthwhile. But schools are a special place, and teachers are special people with a special role and function. Teachers should not be in the business of sympathetically articulating or propagating the commonplace; they should not limit their endeavours to laying out alternatives in the hope that pupils might choose among them freely and autonomously; and they ought to replace *laissez-faire* attitudes with interventionism. As Peters (1966) has indicated, teachers cannot:

> say that what people want to do is their own affair, provided
> that they do no damage to others or interfere with their liberty.
> To adopt this *laissez-faire* attitude in a school would be to

abdicate as an educator. Caretakers, maybe, can adopt such an attitude, but not teachers. (p. 194)

The agency of highly educated and morally concerned teachers, at one and the same time teachers and pupils serving the people whilst resisting relations of ascribed status, could be central to the enterprise of rational social reconstruction based on the promotion of human excellences and genuine participatory democracy: for such teachers would be well placed to open and adapt schooling and the curriculum for those oppressed groups that do not have an established history of benefiting from them. This position and form of agency, however, will not be simply handed to teachers. Taking it up initially, and then maintaining it at a significant level, are matters for contest and struggle.

What Can Be Achieved?

I noted at the beginning of this book that the present history of teachers is one of decreased status and control, loss of autonomy, destruction of health, worsening of conditions conducive to lowering of morale, and subjugation to increasing external control of schooling and curricula. Numerous accounts from many countries have detailed meddling with teachers' roles in attempts to commodify education and make schools instrumental agents of types of market-driven and market-managed social arrangements. Within this context teachers *are* becoming the agents and/ or puppets of commercial and political interests many steps removed from the classroom (and thus, according to Gibson, should not be enjoying this version of schooling either); and they are losing power and control over the basic conditions of their work, which is also becoming newly situated in changing social and technical divisions of labour. In the face of this situation teachers have basically two options. They can either allow themselves to be drawn along in the general prevailing flow, or else they can beat against that flow and pull in a different direction. The choice is one of either being manipulated, or else taking a vanguard role.

There is good reason, in the present context of the appropriation of educational discourse and schooling practice within a techno-rationalist and market-oriented agenda, to suggest that teachers ought to contest the present situation and seek, as intellectuals, to control rather than merely manage the schooling process. However, it is necessary to keep both feet on reality here and to place the prescriptions being made into the context of what teachers actually can achieve. This is hardly the place to detail a full programmatic agenda for teachers; and instead of engaging in so ambitious an enterprise I want simply to indicate certain broad areas in which teachers might profitably direct their concerns and energies. In doing so I continue to take heed of a point made at the beginning of chapter 3; namely that what teachers can achieve as an identifiable interest group is related to the level and control of power that they have in the arena of struggle. Thus underlying all of the following suggestions is a fundamental recognition of the need for teachers to continually seek to increase their power and influence in educational policy and debate.

First, teachers would do well to protect their profession, and especially the credentialling aspect of it, given that we need better, not worse, educated teachers. The growing literature, especially from the UK (for example, O'Hear, 1988; Lawlor, 1990) and New Zealand (for example, Lough *et al*, 1990), along with increasing practices relating to teacher-education, teacher-employment and teacher-promotion, such as the movement from tertiary-based initial teacher education to school-based teacher training, appointing school principals from beyond the ranks of teachers, and recruiting teachers with minimal or no formal training, present ominous warnings of just how seriously teacher education and credentialling are under threat.

Secondly, teachers would do well to seek greater control of schooling, and especially increased control of the curriculum; and then take active responsibility for formulating not only the substantive curriculum but also the political and personal goals sought through it (which does not mean acting in isolation from parents, pupils, employers and other legitimately interested parties). Gaining greater control of schooling may, on the face of it, appear to be already well under way, given that in much of the Western world a major transformation in the mode of providing government schooling is occurring in which, under the banners of 'decentralization', 'devolution', 'consumer choice' and 'local management of schooling', increasing decision-making and day-to-day management is being determined by schools and/or local regions, while less of this is being devised and deployed from a single central government edifice. However, as I have argued elsewhere (Harris, 1994), this process, more specifically and despite its supporting discourse, offers greater choices of a limited sort, only to some people, and even then within more tightly bound externally contrived parameters. It is devolution within a context where the educational aspect of schooling is itself limited or 'restricted' in the sense that providing it for some requires denying it to others. It is also devolution in a context where the state, even when employing the discourse of liberalism, is clearly and overtly seeking to maintain and increase control over the knowledge and conclusions to be legitimated for future generations (through National Curricula, etc.), and thus to construct and promote knowledge and values which foreclose certain forms of critical thought and action, while leaving it to devolved power [1] to promulgate those conditions of schooling in which the success of individual schools and pupils is achieved at the expense of pupils and schools that cannot compete meaningfully for the finite resources available and the finite rewards ultimately on offer. In that context local management translates not into diversified and expanded education of autonomous critical citizens constructing a democratic future, but into competition between schools which increases some pupils' life chances at the expense of other pupils, with such competition and outcomes endorsed, controlled and fostered by the state. In this process schooling becomes a divisive agency where 'education' is commonly and selectively reduced to engendering attitudes and skills relating to compliance, and in which teachers, having been given more power in the day-to-day legitimation and dissemination of more tightly held state-legitimated knowledge and values, find their effectiveness being gauged in terms of successfully conserving the overall social system allegedly being opened up for involved determination. This in turn tends to de-professionalize teachers through reducing their role in curriculum formulation, while stressing their functionary status in the school rather than the need for them to be better and more critically educated (and thus be better placed to identify and be critical of the political-ideological role of the state itself).

Given that transformative and reconstructive activity would be easier to undertake where the state had less control of legitimated knowledge and a less-easy path in 'social engineering', teachers would do well to avoid rather than cooperate with these sorts of socially divisive and economically-manipulative policies and practices. If teachers are to go along with increased local control and management of schooling they would do better to direct their involvement to curriculum and broad policy issues rather than the trivia of day-to-day management, book-keeping or educationally-alien practices associated narrowly with things like promoting the school as a business within the community, or broadly with producing divisions related to unequal social and production relations. They would do even better still to combine and share their particular skills with, and at the same time listen to and learn from, the community the school serves. This is little if anything removed from the role and function of the organic intellectual.

Finally, but by no means exhaustively, teachers would do well to oppose their role being crafted for them by political and managerial bureaucrats and ideologues. That, however, reads far too easily, and requires at least a modicum of detailing here.

There are three broad things that teachers might do in opposing the political and ideological redefinition of their role, which is basically an exercise in proletarianizing teachers through the attempt to create and legitimate a deskilled and deprofessionalized image of teaching.

The first is to fight for those conditions that can be preserved and attained. While the global process of continuing (but not continuous) proletarianization may be near enough to inevitable while capitalism remains the dominant mode of production, teachers can affect the speed and intensity with which it affects them by, among other things, the amount of resistance they put forward in relation to the degree to which any particular issue is amenable to resistance at any particular time. This itself depends heavily on historical factors; and some times are more favourable than others for achieving tangible results. But teachers can take initiatives, make advances, and actually win out in certain issues, and many such gains should be expected in a dialectical historical process. The success, in April 1993, of the challenge by teachers in the UK to having to administer to all 7 and 14-year-old children classroom tests imposed by a government department (a challenge upheld by the Court of Appeal) bears testimony to the fact that major issues can be won, especially if fought for on a strong united front. Gains can also be more easily held where teachers have strong public and parental support, thus emphasizing the need for teachers to work with, and be respected as professionals by, the communities in which they work. In this type of context teachers can defend things related to their professional function, up to a point, and successfully oppose matters such as individual contracting, employment of unregistered teachers, appointment of non-teaching managers to executive positions in schools, silencing of teachers' voices on educational committees, and so on. It would, however, almost certainly be the case that the ability of teachers to take initiatives, let alone to defend conditions and oppose unwelcome changes, would decrease dramatically within the rationalized conditions (especially those that remove the propensity for collective bargaining and substitute individual contracts in its place) which are commonly being proposed and which in some places have already been implemented.

The second thing teachers might do is to assist, where possible, in the larger struggles against proletarianization which are less likely to be won short of an unlikely social revolution. Teachers may have the sorts of power indicated above but, realistically if regrettably, they are relatively powerless to directly influence other types of imposed conditions, like large-scale cuts in government spending on schools, and especially major restructuring programs which begin far outside of schooling and are themselves part of a broader microeconomic restructuring within the state. This does not mean that teachers can do absolutely nothing at all. Working to reconstruct future social relations, or even simply spreading awareness of what the new restructuring actually means for the education of children both individually and collectively, may not be totally without merit and effect. It is important to recognize here that the familiar context of experience and struggle, the insulated nation-state, has gone, and with it have gone the centralized bureaucracies that once weighed so heavily on public service as to stifle rather than stimulate it. These bureaucratic structures were justifiably despised, and while it may be unwise to completely abolish a centralized form of state articulation concerned with equitably resourcing the schooling system, their reestablishment might best not be advocated. As Anna Yeatman (1991) reminds us, political activity has to be forward-looking, requiring 'of us new learning and new vision' capable of contextualizing social democratic values in a transnational, multicultural and multiracial setting (p. 7). With this new learning, Yeatman concludes:

> We can then proceed to effectively contest the way in which economic competition agendas are subjecting public values to private values with a new and relevant vision of citizenship, democracy and justice. (*ibid*)

It need hardly be added that teachers of the sort I am advocating ought be well placed to form, develop and promote the sort of new vision required.

The third major task for teachers in opposing the redefinition of their role is to contest the appropriation of educational discourse by the particular vision of economic rationalism and then to regain control of that discourse themselves.

The appropriation of educational discourse by economic rationalism has been well charted and documented, and we are becoming all too familiar these days with talk of the education industry, marketing schools and education, supply, demand, effective school management to gain a competitive edge in order to enhance leverage, and so on; just as we are also beginning to become familiar with new practices and values constructed in terms of that discourse. The discourse is particularly seductive and needs some consideration here.

Economic rationalism has gained its wide popularity, I believe, not so much on account of any irrefutable internal logic which, as I have argued elsewhere (Harris, 1991, pp. 82–4) it certainly does not have, but rather because it has been successfully presented and situated as a viable modern successor to liberal idealism. It has given the appearance of respecting the underlying 'educational' goals of liberal idealism, and also of largely overcoming the idealist dilemma regarding offering 'real education' within the context of having to school everybody, simply by legitimating the instrumental nature of schooling. It has also appropriated the central materialist point that schooling is basically an intermediary institution between the family and the labour market, without taking on the less popular complex materialist justification for this or any other of its conclusions; and it has then actively promoted the idea that schools can be more socially and economically efficient by tying in more closely with the labour market through teaching the vocational skills and knowledge required by future workers. In addition to this it has carefully and deliberately appropriated recent radical critiques of education (as the 1987 New Zealand Treasury document clearly reveals) in order both to attempt to defuse any similar critiques directed against itself and to show, ostensibly in its own way and off its own bat, how traditional idealist liberal education has failed to achieve its goals. Economic rationalism has thus been set up as a newly evolved, modern yet traditionally grounded, robust, expert, disinterested viable alternative discourse. It has become constructed as a form of analysis allegedly well suited to contextualizing and understanding education in a changed modern era, while at the same time managing to be critical of past legitimated approaches without totally alienating those traditional intellectuals who championed liberal idealism, and without taking on the perceived 'excesses' and political connotations and associations of materialism. Its success in achieving this has enabled it to effectively 'naturalize' education as an industry and contextualize schools as competitors in some educational market place.

The success of the purveyors of economic rationalism in this area, however, and notwithstanding the fact that times and economic circumstances have changed, in no way establishes that economic rationalism is capable of providing the robust analysis to best serve us to handle the changes and problems we presently face, in education or in sociopolitical life in general. Numerous commentators have shown that economic rationalism might be an effective ideological weapon, but that it is a poor analytic tool which hardly offers the most authoritative of explanations. There are problems with both its logic and its analytic value, which invite challenge on epistemic grounds (Harris, 1991); but as a field of discourse it is itself open to far more global interrogation. The question Grace (1988, pp. 7–8) sees as our entitlement to ask of any field of discourse, namely 'Where is it leading us?', is particularly pertinent to economic rationalism.

Economic rationalism, given its philosophic grounding, its wide-ranging social application and its particular form of psychological appeal, is a discourse with enormous power to include and exclude agents, and legitimate and delegitimate practice. To fail to challenge it in the present moment could be to allow those with narrow techno-rational interests, and who analyze education with the same categories and within the same framework as they analyze small business and major industries, to create a discourse which effectively closes off opposing discourse and progressively excludes those 'outside' it from participation. To then help legitimate such a discourse by silence, reverence or ignorance, could be to acquiesce in bringing about one's own eventual impotence as a commentator on, and agent within, the field of education. But there is more to it than this.

There is dangerous potential within the analytic categories of economic rationalism to present major forms of critical thought, along with liberal education itself, as luxuries barely affordable in the present economic and political conditions. There is also the potential to establish the ideological position of identifying certain criticism and modes of thought as no longer valid or relevant, or even as the irrational product of the disaffected. It could thus turn out that the discourse of economic rationalism, if allowed to guide the agenda even just for the reconstruction of the provision of education and schooling, might bring about the progressive silencing within society of those best able to subject that discourse and its wider sociopolitical ramifications to critical scrutiny; in much the same way that removing certain forms of critical thought, mainly sociology and philosophy, from initial teacher education (on alleged grounds of efficiency) could serve to silence particular potential criticism of education from within the field of educational practice itself. It would therefore be wise for all who are concerned with education, not only those directly affected, to neither remain ignorant of that potential, nor to endorse or accept economic rationalism as the natural, logical or best modern alternative to liberal idealism, but rather to enter the political arena of critical scholarly challenge. Again a vanguard role for the teacher-as-intellectual beckons.

Conclusion

What is being suggested here for teachers may be difficult, but it is neither impossible nor strictly utopian. Schools, along with universities and other tertiary institutions involved with the education of teachers are public spheres as well as historical constructions serving historically expressed needs of societies; and regardless of the way they are presently suffering reconstitution and technocratic and managerial restructuring, they continue to bear some ideological commitment to individual and social betterment, and they are likely to remain institutions in which teachers shall retain at least some agency in the key area of the transmission of knowledge. While this agency is significantly maintained it thus remains possible for teachers to adopt the function of intellectuals (a possibility not extinguished by the structuralist framework of the argument in this book) and, within the spaces created by the contradictions inherent in the present phase of historic development, to resist intellectual and managerial incorporation, to resist becoming mere managers of day-to-day activities imposed from beyond the school, and to redefine their role within counterhegemonic practice. They can, through their discourse and interventionary practice in the ideological and political determinants of schooling, promote empowerment, autonomy and democracy. They can work towards extending human capacities and overcoming wastage of human resources and potential. They can, through determining and articulating the form and content of the curriculum and the purposes and conditions of schooling, and then through their classroom activity, take a leading role in constructing a future built on and celebrating the participatory power of the autonomous person — a future our children might face with some excitement rather than turn away from. Without such activity on the part of teachers there will remain an ever-present risk that the purposes and practices of schooling could be directed towards lesser ends.

Note

1   Lingard (1990) usefully refers to this as devolution of action rather than power.

Select Bibliography

ALEXANDER, D. (1988) 'The new class: Reconstituting a neglected social construct', *Unicorn*, 12, (1), pp. 24–9.

ALEXANDER, R. *et al* (1992) *Curriculum Organisation and Classroom Practice in Primary Schools*, London: DES.

ALTHUSSER, L. (1984) 'Ideology and ideological state apparatuses', in *Essays on Ideology*, London: Verso.

AMIN, S. (1974) *Accumulation on a World Scale*, New York: Monthly Review Press.

ANDERSON, R. (1986). 'The genesis of clinical supervision', in SMYTH, J. (Ed.) *Learning About Teaching Through Clinical Supervision*, London: Croom Helm.

ANGUS, L. (1986) *Schooling, the School Effectiveness Movement and Educational Reform*, Geelong: Deakin University Press.

ANGUS, L. (1989) 'Democratic participation and administrative control in education', *International Journal of Educational Management*, 3, (2), pp. 20–6.

ANGUS, L. and RIZVI, F. (1989) 'Power and the politics of participation', *Journal of Educational Administration and Foundations*, 4, (1), pp. 6–23.

APPLE, M. (1983) 'Work, gender and teaching', *Teachers College Record*, 84, (3), pp. 611–28.

APPLE, M. (1986a) 'Curriculum conflict in the United States' in HARNETT, A. and NAISH, M. (Eds), *Education and Society Today*, London: Falmer Press.

APPLE, M. (1986b) *Teachers and Texts*, New York: Routledge and Kegan Paul.

APPLE, M. (1987) 'Producing inequality: Ideology and economy in the national reports on education', *Educational Studies* (USA) 18, (2), pp. 195–220.

APPLE, M. (1989) 'How equality has been redefined in the conservative restoration', in SECADA, W. (Ed.), *Equity in Education*, London: Falmer Press.

APPLE, M. (1992a) 'The politics of official knowledge: Does a National Curriculum make sense?', The John Dewey Lecture presented to AERA Symposium, San Francisco, April.

APPLE, M. (1992b) *The Politics of Official Knowledge*, New York: Routledge.

APPLE, M. and CHRISTIAN-SMITH, L. (Eds) (1991) *The Politics of the Textbook*, London: Routledge.

ARNOLD, M. (1963) *Culture and Anarchy*, Cambridge: Cambridge University Press.

ARNOLD, M. (1964) *Essays in Criticism*, London: J.M. Dent.

ARNOLD, M. (1967) 'Literature and science' in GRIBBLE, J. (Ed.) *Matthew Arnold*, London: Collier Macmillan.

ARNOT, M. and WEINER, G. (Eds) (1987) *Gender and the Politics of Schooling*, London: Hutchinson.

ARONOWITZ, S. and GIROUX, H. (1985) *Education Under Siege*, Massachusetts: Bergin and Garvey.

ASHTON, D.N., MAGUIRE, M. and SPILSBURY, M. (1990) *Restructuring the Labour Market: The Implications for Youth*, London: Macmillan.

AUERBACH, P. (1988) *Competition: The Economics of Industrial Change*, Oxford: Blackwell.

AUSTRALIAN BUREAU OF STATISTICS (1987) *Labour Force Status and Educational Attainment*, Cat. 6235.

AUSTRALIAN EDUCATION COUNCIL REVIEW COMMITTEE (1991) *Young People's Participation in Post-compulsory Education and Training* (Finn Report), Canberra: Australian Government Publishing Service.

BALL, S. (1990a) 'Education, inequality and school reform: Values in crisis! An inaugural lecture', Centre for Educational Studies, King's College, London.

BALL, S. (1990b) *Politics and Policy Making in Education: Explorations in Policy Sociology*, London: Routledge.

BALL, S. (1990c) *Markets, Morality and Equality in Education*, London: Tufnell Press.

BALL, S. and GOODSON, I. (Eds) (1985) *Teachers' Lives and Careers*, London: Falmer Press.

BARLOW, K. (1989) 'The White Paper and restructuring the academic labour market', *Australian Universities' Review*, 32, (1), pp. 30–7.

BARNET, R. (1983) 'The decline of corporate myths', in CROUGH, G., WHEELWRIGHT, T. and WILSHIRE, T. (Eds) *Australian and World Capitalism*, Ringwood: Penguin.

BARON, S. *et al* (1981) *Unpopular Education*, London: Hutchinson.

BARRETT, E., BARTON, L., FURLONG, J., GALVIN, C., MILES, S. and WHITTY, G. (1992) *Initial Teacher Education in England and Wales — A Topography*, London: University of London, Goldsmiths' College Modes of Teacher Education Project.

BARTLETT, L., KNIGHT, J. and LINGARD, R. (1991) 'Corporate federalism and the reform of teacher education in Australia,' *Journal of Education Policy*, 6, (1), pp. 85–90.

BARTLETT, L., LINGARD, R. and KNIGHT, J. (1992) 'Restructuring teacher education in Australia', *British Journal of Sociology of Education*, 13, (1), pp. 19–36.

BARTON, L., POLLARD, A. and WHITTY, G. (1992) 'Experiencing CATE: The impact of accreditation upon initial training institutions in England', *Journal of Education For Teaching*, 18, (1), pp. 41–5.

BASTIAN, A., FRUCHTER, N., GITTEL, M., GREER, G. and HASKINS, K. (1986) *Choosing Equality: The Case for Democratic Schooling*, Philadelphia: Temple University Press.

BATES, R. (1990) 'Education policy and the new cult of efficiency', in MIDDLETON, S., CODD, J. and JONES, A. (Eds) *New Zealand Education Policy Today*, Wellington: Allen and Unwin, pp. 40–52.

BEILHARZ, P. (1986) 'The left, the "Accord" and the future of socialism', *Thesis Eleven*, 13, pp. 5–21.

BEILHARZ, P. (1987) 'Political theory and policy making in education', *The Australian and New Zealand Journal of Sociology*, 23, (3), pp. 388–406.

BENNIS, W. (1968) 'The coming death of bureaucracy', in ATHOS, A. and COFFEY, R. (Ed.) *Behaviour in organisations*, New Jersey: Prentice Hall.

BEREITER, C. (1972) 'Moral alternatives to education', *Interchange*, 3, (1).

BEREITER, C. (1973) *Must we Educate?*, New Jersey: Prentice Hall.

BERG, I. (1970) *Education and Jobs: The Great Training Robbery*, New York: Praeger.

BERLAK, A. and BERLAK, H. (1981) *Dilemmas of Schooling: Teaching and Social Change*, London: Methuen.

BERNSTEIN, B. (1973) 'Education cannot compensate for society', in RAYNOR, J. and HARDEN, J. (Eds) *Equality and City Schools*, London: Routledge and Kegan Paul.

BEST, M. (1990) *The New Competition: Institutions of Industrial Restructuring*, Cambridge: Polity Press.

BEVERLEY, J. (1982) 'Higher education and capitalist crisis', in DERBER, D. (Ed.) *Professionals and Workers: Mental Labor in Advanced Capitalism*, Boston: G.K. Hall, pp. 100–20.

BIRCH, I. and SMART, D. (1989) 'Economic rationalism and the politics of education in Australia', *Journal of Education Policy*, 4, (5), pp. 137–51.

BLACKBURN, R. and MANN, M. (1979) *The Working Class in the Labour Market*, London: Macmillan.

BLOCK, F. (1990) *Postindustrial Possibilities: A Critique of Economic Discourse*, Berkeley: California University Press.

BLOOM, A. (1987) *The Closing of the American Mind*, New York: Simon and Schuster.

BLUER, R. and CARMICHAEL, L. (1991) 'Award restructuring in teaching', *Unicorn*, 17, (1), pp. 24–9.

BOOTH, M., FURLONG, V.J. and WILKIN, M. (1990) *Partnership in Initial Teacher Training*, London: Cassell.

BOSTON, J. (1987) 'Future directions for New Zealand universities: Some reflections on the market liberal approach', *New Zealand Journal of Educational Studies*, 22, pp. 175–87.

BOSTON, J. (1988) 'Democratic theory, devolution and accountability', in MARTIN, J. and HARPER, J. (Eds) *Devolution and Accountability*, Wellington: New Zealand Institute of Public Administration, pp. 46–71.

BOSTON, J. (1991) 'The theoretical underpinnings of public sector restructuring', in BOSTON, J., MARTIN, J., PALLOT, J. and WALSH, P. (Eds), *Reshaping the State: New Zealand's Bureaucratic Revolution*, Auckland: Oxford University Press.

BOURDIEU, P. and PASSERON, J-C. (1977) *Reproduction: in Education, Society and Culture*, London: Sage.

BOWE, R. and BALL, S. (1991) 'Doing what comes naturally: An exploration of LMS in one secondary school', Centre for Educational Studies, King's College, London.

BOWERS, C.A. (1984a) 'The problem of individualism and community in neo-marxist educational thought', *Teachers College Record*, 85, (3).

BOWERS, C.A. (1984b) *The Promise of Theory: Education and the Politics of Cultural Change*, New York: Longman.

BOWLES, S. and GINTIS, H. (1976) *Schooling in Capitalist America*, New York: Basic Books.

BOWLES, S. and GINTIS, H. (1987) *Democracy and Capitalism*, New York: Basic Books.

BRAVERMAN, H. (1975) *Labor and Monopoly Capital: The Degradation of Work in the Twentieth Century*, New York: Monthly Review Press.

BREDO, E. (1988) 'Choice, constraint and community', in BOYD, W. and KERCHNER, C. (Eds), *The Politics of Excellence and Choice in Education*, London: Falmer Press.

BRITTAN, S. (1988) *A Restatement of Economic Liberalism*, London: Macmillan.

BROADFOOT, P. *et al* (1988) 'What professional responsibility means to teachers: National contexts and classroom constants', *British Journal of Sociology of Education*, 9, (3), pp. 265–87.

BROWN, P. (1987) *Schooling Ordinary Kids*, London: Tavistock.

BROWN, P. and LAUDER, H. (1991a) 'Education, economy and society: An introduction to a new agenda', in BROWN, P. and LAUDER, H. (Eds) *Education for Economic Survival: From Fordism to Post-Fordism?*, London: Routledge.

BROWN, P. and LAUDER, H. (1991b) 'Education, economy and social change', *International Journal of Sociology of Education*, 1, pp. 65–85.

BRUGGER, B. and JAENSCH, D. (1986) *Australian Politics: Theory and Practice*, Sydney: Allen & Unwin.

BRYAN, D. (1989) 'Whose balance of payments?', *Journal of Australian Political Economy*, 24, pp. 56–76.

BUCHANAN, J. and WAGNER, R. (1977) *Democracy in Deficit*, New York: Academic Press.

BULBECK, C. (1983) 'Economists as midwives of capitalist ideology', in WHEELWRIGHT, E. and BUCKLEY, K. (Eds) *Essays in the Political Economy of Australian Capitalism*, Volume 5, Brookvale: Australia & New Zealand Book Co., pp. 101–18.

BURCHELL, D. (1986) 'Tertiary education for sale', *Australian Society*, December, pp. 22–4.

BURGESS, J. (1989) 'Productivity: A worker problem?', *Journal of Australian Political Economy*, 24, pp. 23–8.

BURKE, G. (1991) 'Teachers and economic policy', in MACLEAN, R. and McKENZIE, P. (Eds) *Australian Teachers' Careers*, Melbourne: Australian Council for Educational Research.

BURKE, G. and RUMBERGER, R. (Eds) (1987) *The Future Impact of Work and Technology on Education*, London: Falmer Press.

CALDWELL, B. and SPINKS, J. (1988) *The Self-Managing School*, London: Falmer Press.

CARLSON, D. (1987) 'Teachers as political actors', *Harvard Education Review*, 57, (3), pp. 283–306.

CARNOY, M. and LEVIN, H.M. (1985) *Schooling and Work in the Democratic State*, Stanford, C.A.: Stanford University Press.

CARR, W. (1987) 'Critical theory and educational studies', *Journal of Philosophy of Education*, 21, (2), pp. 287–95.

CARR, W. and KEMMIS, S. (1986) *Becoming Critical: Education, Knowledge and Action Research*, Geelong: Deakin University Press.

Teachers: Constructing the Future

Teachers: Constructing the Future

CASTELLS M. and HENDERSON, J. (Eds) (1987) *Global Restructuring and Territorial Development*, London: Sage.

CASTLES, F. (1988) *Australian Public Policy and Economic Vulnerability: A Comparative and Historical Perspective*, Sydney: Allen and Unwin.

CAWSON, A. and SAUNDERS, P. (1983) 'Corporatism, competitive politics and class struggle,' in R. KING (Ed.) *Capital and Politics*, London: Routledge and Kegan Paul.

CERNY, P. (1990) *The Changing Architecture of Politics: Structure, Agency and the Future of the State*, London: Sage.

CHAPMAN, J., ANGUS, L. and BURKE, G. (Eds) (1991) *Improving the Quality of Australian Schools*, Melbourne: Australian Council for Educational Research.

CHOMSKY, N. (1971) *American Power and the New Mandarins*, Harmondsworth: Penguin.

CHOMSKY, N. (1988) *Power and Ideology*, Boston: South End Press.

CHOMSKY, N. (1989) *Necessary Illusions: Thought Control in Democratic Societies*, Boston: South End Press.

CHOMSKY, N. and HERMAN, E.S. (1988) *Manufacturing Consent: the Political Economy of the Mass Media*, New York: Pantheon.

CHUBB, J. and MOE, T. (1990) *Politics, Markets and America's Schools*, Washington: The Brookings Institution.

CICOUREL, A.V. and KITSUSE, J.I. (1963) *The Education Decision-Makers*, New York: Bobbs-Merill.

CODD, J. (1988) 'The construction and deconstruction of educational policy documents', *Journal of Education*, 3, (3), pp. 235–47.

CODD, J. and GORDON, L. (1991) 'School charters: The contractualist state and education policy', *New Zealand Journal of Educational Studies*, 26, (1), pp. 21–34.

CODD J., GORDON, L. and HARKER, R. (1990) 'Education and the role of the state: Devolution and control post-Picot', in LAUDER, H. and WYLIE, C. (Eds), *Towards Successful Schooling*, London: Falmer Press, pp. 15–32.

CODD, J., HARKER, R. and NASH, R. (1990) 'Education, Politics and the Economic Crisis,' in CODD, J., HARKER, R. and NASH, R. (Eds), *Political Issues in New Zealand Education*, Palmerston North: Dunmore Press, pp. 7–22.

COLE, M. (Ed.) (1987) *Schooling in Capitalist America Ten Years On*, London: Falmer Press.

COLEMAN, J. *et al* (1966) *Equality of Educational Opportunity*, Washington: US Government Printing Office.

CONNELL, R. (1985) *Teachers' Work*, Sydney: Allen and Unwin.

CONNELL, R. (1989) 'Curriculum politics, hegemony and strategies for social change', *New Education*, 11, (2), pp. 63–71.

CONNELL, R. (1990) 'The state, gender and sexual politics,' *Theory and Society*, 19, pp. 507–44.

CONNELL, R. *et al* (1982) *Making the Difference*, Sydney: Allen and Unwin.

CONNORS, L. (1989) *Futures for Schooling in Australia: Nationalisation, Privatisation or Unification?*, The Australian College of Education, Occasional paper No. 13, Deakin, ACT.

CONSIDINE, M. (1988) 'The corporate managerial framework as administrative science: A Critique', *Australian Journal of Public Administration*, 47, (1), pp. 4–19.

COOPER, B. (1990) 'Local school reform in Great Britain and the United States: Points of comparison — points of departure', *Educational Review*, 42, (2), pp. 133–49.

DALE, R. (1982) 'Education and the capitalist state', in APPLE, M. (Ed.) *Cultural and Economic Reproduction in Education*, London: Routledge and Kegan Paul.

DALE, R. (1989) *The State and Education Policy*, Milton Keynes: Open University Press.

DAVID, A. and WHEELWRIGHT, T. (1989) *The Third Wave: Australia and World Capitalism*, Sutherland: Left Book Club.

DAVIS, G., WELLER, P. and LEWIS, C. (Eds) (1989) *Corporate Management in Australian Government*, Melbourne: Macmillan.

DAWKINS, J. (1987) *Higher Education: A Policy Discussion Paper*, Canberra: Australian Government Publishing Service.

DAWKINS, J. (1988a) *Higher Education: A Policy Statement*, Canberra: Australian Government Publishing Service.

DAWKINS, J. (1988b) *Strengthening Australia's Schools*, Canberra: Australian Government Publishing Service.

DEPARTMENT OF EDUCATION AND SCIENCE (1987) *Grant Maintained Schools: A Consultation Paper*, London: HMSO.

DEPARTMENT OF EDUCATION AND SCIENCE (1992) *Reform of Initial Teacher Training: A Consultation Document*, London: HMSO.

DUNLEAVY, P. and O'LEARY, B. (1987) *Theories of the State: The Politics of Liberal Democracy*, London: Macmillan.

DWYER, P. *et al* (1984) *Confronting School and Work*, Sydney: George Allen and Unwin.

ECONOMIC PLANNING AND ADVISORY COUNCIL (1990) *The Size and Efficiency of the Public Sector*, Council paper No.44, Canberra: Australian Government Publishing Service.

ELIOT, T.S. (1967) *Notes Toward the Definition of Culture*, London: Faber.

ESPING-ANDERSEN, G. (1985a) *Politics Against Markets*, Princeton: Princeton University Press.

Esping-Andersen, G. (1985b) 'Power and distributional regimes', *Politics and Society*, 14, (2), pp. 223–56.

Esping-Andersen, G. (1990) *The Three Worlds of Welfare Capitalism*, Princeton, N.J.: Princeton University Press.

Evatt Research Centre (1989) *State of Siege: Renewal or Privatisation for Australian State Public Services?*, Sydney: Pluto Press.

Fay, B. (1975) *Social Theory and Political Practice*, London: Allen and Unwin.

Fay, B. (1977) 'How people change themselves: The relationship between critical theory and its audience', in Ball, T. (Ed.) *Political Theory and Praxis: New Perspectives*, Minneapolis: University of Minnesota Press, pp. 200–33.

Fay, B. (1987) *Critical Social Science: Liberation and its Limits*, Oxford: Polity Press.

Feuer, L.W. (Ed.) (1972) *Marx and Engels: Basic Writings on Politics and Philosophy*, London: Fontana Books.

Fisher, D. (1991) 'Privatization and education: Some reflections on changes in Canada', in Gordon, L. and Codd, J. (Eds) *Education Policy and the Changing Role of the State*, Palmerston North: Delta Studies in Education, pp. 42–57.

Flinders, D. (1988) 'Teacher isolation and the new reform', *Journal of Curriculum and Supervision*, 4, (1), pp. 17–29.

Forgacs, D. (1988) *A Gramsci Reader*, London: Lawrence and Wishart.

Foucault, M. (1977) 'Intellectuals and power' in Bouchard, D. (Ed.) *Language, Counter-Memory, Practice*, N.Y.: Cornell University Press, pp. 205–17.

Foucault, M. (1979) *Discipline and Punish: The Birth of the Prison*, Harmondsworth: Penguin.

Freeland, J. (1986) 'Australia: The search for a new educational settlement', in Sharp, R. (Ed.), *Capitalist Crisis and Schooling: Comparative Studies in the Politics of Education*, Melbourne: Macmillan.

Freeland, J. (1991) 'Equality of what and equality for whom?', in Chapman, J. *et al* (Eds), *Improving the Quality of Australian Schools*, Melbourne: Australian Council for Educational Research.

Freeland, J. and Sharp, R. (1981) 'The Williams report on education, training and employment: The decline and fall of Karmelot', *Intervention*, 14, pp. 54–79.

Freire, P. (1972a) *Pedagogy of the Oppressed*, Harmondsworth: Penguin.

Freire, P. (1972b) *Cultural Action For Freedom*, Harmondsworth: Penguin.

Frobel, F., Heinrichs, J. and Kreye, O. (1980) *The New International Division of Labour*, Cambridge: Cambridge University Press.

FULLAN, M. (1982) *The Meaning of Educational Change*, New York: Teachers College Press.

GALBRAITH, J. (1967) *The New Industrial State*, London: Hamish Hamilton.

GAMBLE, A. (1986) 'The political economy of freedom', in LEVITAS, R. (Ed.) *The Ideology of the New Right*, Cambridge: Polity Press.

GERRITSEN, R. (1986) 'The necessity of "corporatism": The case of the Hawke Labor government', *Politics*, 21, (1), pp. 45–54.

GIBSON, R. (1984) *Structuralism and Education*, London: Hodder and Stoughton.

GILLIGAN, C. (1982) *In a Different Voice*, Cambridge: Harvard University Press.

GIROUX, H. (1983) *Theory and Resistance in Education*, Boston, MA: Bergin and Garvey.

GIROUX, H. (1987) 'Educational reform and the politics of teacher empowerment', *New Education*, 9, (1&2), pp. 3–13.

GITLIN, A. and SMYTH, J. (1989) *Teacher Evaluation: Educative Alternatives*, London: Falmer Press.

GOODMAN, J. (1984) 'Reflection and teacher education: A case study and theoretical analysis', *Interchange*, 19, pp. 9–26.

GOODMAN, P. (1972) *Compulsory Miseducation*, Harmondsworth: Penguin.

GORDON, D., EDWARDS, R. and REICH, M. (1982) *Segmented Work, Divided Workers: The Historical Transformation of Labor in the United States*, Cambridge: Cambridge University Press.

GORDON, L. (1985) 'Towards emancipation in citizenship education: The case of Afro-American Cultural knowledge', *Theory and Research in Social Education*, 12 (4), pp. 1–23.

GORDON, L. (1992) 'The state, devolution and educational reform in New Zealand', *Journal of Education Policy*, 7, (2), pp. 187–203.

GOULDNER, A. (1954) *Patterns of Industrial Bureaucracy*, New York: Basic Books.

GOULDNER, A. (1979) *The Future of Intellectuals and the Rise of a New Class*, New York: Oxford University Press.

GRACE, G. (1978) *Teachers, Ideology and Control: A Study in Urban Education*, London: Routledge and Kegan Paul.

GRACE, G. (1985) 'Judging teachers: The social and political context of teacher evaluation', *British Journal of Sociology of Education*, 6, (1), pp. 3–16.

GRACE, G. (1987) 'Teachers and the state in Britain: A changing relation', in LAWN, M. and GRACE, G. (Eds), *Teachers: The Culture and Politics of Work*, London: Falmer Press.

GRACE, G. (1988) *Education: Commodity or Public Good?*, Wellington: Victoria University Press.

GRACE, G. (1990) 'Labour and education reform: The crises and settlements of education policy', in HOLLAND, M. and BOSTON, J. (Eds), *The Fourth Labour Government*, 2nd edn, Auckland: Oxford University Press.

GRACE, G. (1991) 'The new right and the challenge to educational research', *Cambridge Journal of Education*, 21, (3), pp. 265–75.

GRAMSCI, A. (1976) *Selections From the Prison Notebooks*, (Q. Hoare and G. Nowell Smith, Eds), London: Lawrence and Wishart.

GRAVES, N. (Ed.) (1990) *Initial Teacher Education: Policies and Progress*, London: Kogan Page.

GUMBERT, E.B. (Ed.) (1988) *Making the Future*, Georgia: Georgia State University Press.

GUTMAN, A. (1988) 'Distributing public education', in GUTMAN, A. (Ed.), *Democracy and the Welfare State*, Princeton, N.J.: University of Princeton Press.

HABERMAS, J. (1976) *Legitimation Crisis*, London: Heinemann.

HABERMAS, J. (1979) *Communication and the Evolution of Society*, London: Heinemann.

HALL, S. (1988) *The Hard Road to Renewal: Thatcherism and the Crisis of the Left*, London: Verso.

HALSEY, A. *et al* (Eds) (1961) *Education, Economy and Society*, New York: Free Press.

HALSEY, A., HEATH, A. and RIDGE, J. (1984) 'The political arithmetic of public schools', in WALFORD, G. (Ed.) *British Public Schools: Policy and Practice*, London: Falmer Press.

HANDY, C. and AITKEN, R. (1986) *Understanding Schools as Organisations*, London: Penguin.

HANUSHEK, E.A. (1986) 'The economics of schooling: Production and efficiency in public schools', *Journal of Economic Literature*, 24, pp. 1141–77.

HARKER, R. (1985) 'Schooling and cultural reproduction', in CODD, J., HARKER, R. and NASH, R. (Eds) *Political Issues in New Zealand Education*, Palmerston North: Dunmore Press.

HARRIS K., (1979) *Education and Knowledge*, London: Routledge and Kegan Paul.

HARRIS, K. (1982) *Teachers and Classes*, London: Routledge and Kegan Paul.

HARRIS, K. (1990) 'Empowering teachers: Towards a justification of intervention', *Journal of Philosophy of Education*, 24, (2), pp. 171–83.

HARRIS, K. (1991) 'What role For historians of education in determining the history of education?', *Education Research and Perspectives*, 18, (1), pp. 74–87.

HARRIS, K. (forthcoming) 'Mill, the state and local management of schooling', *Journal of Philosophy of Education*.

HARVARD UNIVERSITY, COMMITTEE ON THE OBJECTIVES OF A GENERAL EDUCATION IN A FREE SOCIETY (1945) *General Education in a Free Society: Report of the Harvard Committee*, Cambridge, MA: Harvard University Press.

HARVEY, D. (1989) *The Conditions of Postmodernity*, Oxford: Blackwell.

HAYEK, F. (1960) *The Constitution of Liberty*, Chicago: University of Chicago Press.

HAYEK, F. (1979) *Law, Legislation and Liberty*, Chicago: University of Chicago Press.

HELD, D. (1980) *Introduction to Critical Theory: Horkheimer to Habermas*, London: Hutchinson.

HELD, D. (1989) *Political Theory and the Modern State*, London: Polity Press.

HENRY, J. (1972) *Essays on Education*, Harmondsworth: Penguin.

HEYDEBRAND, W. (1983) 'Technocratic corporatism: Toward a theory of occupational and organizational transformation', in HALL, R. and QUINN, R. (Eds) *Organizational Theory and Public Policy*, Beverley Hills: Sage, pp. 93–114.

HICKOX, M. and MOORE, R. (1991) 'Education and post-Fordism: A new correspondence?', in BROWN, P. and LAUDER, H. (Eds) *Education for Economic Survival*, London: Routledge.

HILL, D. (1991) *What's Left in Teacher Education: Teacher Education, the Radical Left and Policy Proposals*, London: Tufnell Press.

HILLGATE GROUP (1987) *The Reform of British Education*, London: The Claridge Press.

HIRST, P.H. (1974) *Knowledge and the Curriculum*, London: Routledge and Kegan Paul.

HODGE, R. and KRESS, G. (1988) *Social Semiotics*, Cambridge: Polity Press.

HOPKINS, T. and WALLERSTEIN, E. (1982) *World Systems Analysis: Theory and Method*, Beverley Hills: Sage.

HOWARD, R. (1985) *Brave New Workplace*, Harmondsworth: Penguin Books.

HUGHES, D. and LAUDER, H. (1990) 'Public examinations and the structuring of inequality', in LAUDER, H. and WYLIE, C. (Eds), *Towards Successful Schooling*, London: Falmer Press.

HUTCHINS, R.M. (1953) *The Conflict in Education*, New York: Harper.

ILLICH, I. (1971) *Deschooling Society*, Harmondsworth: Penguin.

JACKSON, N. (1987) 'Skill training in transition: Implications for women', in GASKELL, J. and McLAREN, A. (Eds), *Women in Education: A Canadian Perspective*, Calgary: Detselig.

JACKSON, N. (1990) *Skills Formation and Gender Relations: the Politics of Who Knows What*, Geelong: Deakin University Press.

JACKSON, P. (1968) *Life In the Classrooms*, New York: Holt, Rinehart and Winston.

JEFFREYS, M.C. (1963) *Glaucon*, London: Pitman and Sons.

JENCKS, C. *et al* (1972) *Inequality*, New York: Basic Books.

JENKINS, R. (1986) *Racism and Recruitment: Managers, Organisations and Equal Opportunity in the Labour Market*, Cambridge: Cambridge University Press.

JESSON, B. (1987) *Behind the Mirror Glass: The Growth of Wealth and Power in New Zealand in the Eighties*, Auckland: Penguin.

JESSOP, B., BONNETT, K. and BROMLEY, S. (1990) 'Farewell to Thatcherism?, neo-liberalism and "new times" ', *New Left Review*, 179, pp. 81–102.

JONATHAN, R. (1990) 'State education service or prisoner's dilemma: The "Hidden Hand" as a source of education policy,' *Educational Philosophy and Theory*, 22, (1), pp. 16–24.

JUNOR, A. (1988) 'Australian education reconstructed', *Arena*, 84, pp. 133–40.

KAHN, G. (1990) 'The politics of curriculum innovation', in LAUDER, H. and WYLIE, C. (Eds), *Towards Successful Schooling*, London: Falmer Press.

KANTOR, H. and TYACK, D. (Eds) (1982) *Youth, Work and Schooling*, Stanford: Stanford University Press.

KARIER, C.J. (1973) *Roots of Crisis: American Education in the 20th Century*, Chicago: Rand McNally.

KARMEL, P. (1973) (Chairman) *Schools in Australia. Report by the Interim Committee for the Australian School Commission*, Canberra: Australian Government Publishing Service.

KATZ, M.B. (1971) *Class, Bureaucracy and Schools*, New York: Praeger.

KEDDIE, N. (Ed.) (1973) *Tinker Tailor ... The Myth of Cultural Deprivation*, Harmondsworth: Penguin.

KENNEDY, K. (1988) 'The policy context of curriculum reform in Australia in the 1980s', *Australian Journal of Education*, 32, (3), pp. 357–74.

KENNEDY, M. (1988) 'The new global network of corporate power and the decline of national self-determination', *Contemporary Crises*, 12, pp. 245–76.

KENWAY, J. (1990) *Gender and Education Policy: A Call for New Directions*, Geelong: Deakin University Press.

KENWAY, J. and BLACKMORE, J. (1988) 'Gender and the Green Paper:

Privatisation and Equity', *Australian Universities' Review*, 31, (1), pp. 49–57.

KNIGHT, J., LINGARD, R. and PORTER, P. (1991) 'Re-forming the education industry through award restructuring and the new federalism', *Unicorn*, 17, (3), pp. 133–8.

KNIGHT, J., SMITH, R. and CHANT, D. (1989) 'Reconceptualising the dominant ideology debate: An Australian case study', *Australian and New Zealand Journal of Sociology*, 25, (3), pp. 381–409.

KNIGHT, J., SMITH, R. and SACHS, J. (1990) 'Deconstructing hegemony: Multicultural policy and a populist response', in S. BALL (Ed.), *Foucault and Education: Disciplines and Knowledge*, London: Routledge, pp. 133–52.

KOGAN, M. (1979) *Educational Policies in Perspective: An Appraisal*, Paris: Organization for Economic Co-operation and Development.

KOHN, T. and SCHOOLER, C. (1983) *Work and Personality: An Inquiry into the Impact of Social Stratification*, New Jersey: Ablex.

KORPI, W. (1983) *The Democratic Class Struggle*, London: Routledge and Kegan Paul.

KOZOL, J. (1971) *Death At An Early Age*, Harmondsworth: Penguin.

KRIGE, J. (1981) 'Review of K. Harris', *Education and Knowledge, Radical Philosophy*, 28, pp. 41–3.

KUHN, T. (1962) *The Structure of Scientific Revolutions*, Chicago: University of Chicago Press.

KUMAR, K. (1991) 'New theories of industrial society', in BROWN, P. and LAUDER, H. (Eds), *Education for Economic Survival: From Fordism to Post-Fordism?*, London: Routledge.

LACEY, C. (1988) 'The idea of a socialist education', in LAUDER, H. and BROWN, P. (Eds) *Education In Search of a Future*, London: Falmer Press.

LACLAU, E. and MOUFFE, C. (1985) *Hegemony and Socialist Strategy: Towards a Radical Democratic Politics*, London: Verso.

LAMPERT, M. (1985) 'How do teachers manage to teach? Perspectives on problems in practice', *Harvard Educational Review*, 55, (2), pp. 178–94.

LANE, C. (1989) *Management and Labour in Europe*, Aldershot: Edward Elgar.

LANGE, D. (1988) *Tomorrow's Schools: The Reform of Education Administration in New Zealand*, Wellington: New Zealand Government Printer.

LANKSHEAR, C. (1987) *Literacy, Schooling and Revolution*, London: Falmer Press.

LARRAIN, J. (1979) *The Concept of Ideology*, London: Hutchinson.

LARSON, M. (1980) 'Proletarianization and educated labor', *Theory and Society*, 9, (2), pp. 131–75.

LASH, S. and URRY, J. (1987) *The End of Organised Capitalism*, Cambridge: Polity Press.

LATHER, P. (1986a) 'Issues of validity in openly ideological research: Between a rock and a soft place', *Interchange*, 17, (4), pp. 63–84.

LATHER, P. (1986b) 'Research as praxis', *Harvard Educational Review*, 56, (3), pp. 257–77.

LATHER, P. (1991) *Feminist Research in Education: Within/Against*, Geelong: Deakin University Press.

LAUDER, H. (1987) 'The New Right and educational policy in New Zealand', *New Zealand Journal of Educational Studies*, 22, (1), pp. 3–23.

LAUDER, H. (1988) 'Traditions of socialism and educational policy', in LAUDER, H. and BROWN, P. (Eds), *Education in Search of a Future*, London: Falmer Press.

LAUDER, H. (1990) 'Education, democracy and the crisis of the welfare state', in LAUDER, H. and WYLIE, C. (Eds). *Towards Successful Schooling*, London: Falmer Press, pp. 33–52.

LAUDER, H. (1991) 'Education, democracy and the economy', *British Journal of Sociology of Education*, 12, (4), pp. 417–31.

LAUDER, H. and HUGHES, D. (1990) 'Social inequalities and differences in school outcomes', *New Zealand Journal of Educational Studies*, 25, (1), pp. 37–60.

LAUDER, H. and KHAN, G. (1988) 'Democracy and the effective schools movement', *Qualitative Studies in Education*, 1, pp. 51–68.

LAUDER, H. and WYLIE, C. (Eds) (1990) *Towards Successful Schooling*, London: Falmer Press.

LAUDER, H., BROWN, P. and HUGHES, D. (1990) 'The labour market, educational reform and economic growth', *New Zealand Journal of Industrial Relations*, 15, pp. 203–18.

LAUDER, H., SCOTT, A. and FREEMAN-MOIR, J. (1986) 'What is to be done with radical academic practice?', *Capital and Class*, 29, pp. 83–110.

LAURIE, S.S. (1902) *The Training of Teachers*, Cambridge: Cambridge University Press.

LAWLOR, S. (1990) *Teachers Mistaught: Training in Theories or Education in Subjects?*, London: Centre For Policy Studies.

LAWN, M. (Ed.) (1985) *The Politics of Teacher Unionism*, London: Croom Helm.

LAWN, M., and GRACE, G. (Eds) (1987) *Teachers: The Culture and Politics of Work*, London: Falmer Press.

LAWN, M. and OZGA, J. (1988) 'The educational worker? A reassessment of teachers', in OZGA, J. (Ed.) *Schoolwork: Approaches to the Labour Process of Teaching*, Milton Keynes: Open University Press.

LEAVIS, F.R. (1930) *Mass Civilisation and Minority Culture*, Cambridge: Minority Press.

LEAVIS, F.R. (1940) 'Sketch For an English School', *Scrutiny*, IX, pp. 98–120.

LEVIN, H. (1987) 'Improving productivity through education and technology', in BURKE, G. and RUMBERGER, R. (Eds) *The Future Impact of Technology on Work and Education*, London: Falmer Press, pp. 194–214.

LEVIN, H. and RUMBERGER, R. (1983) 'The low-skill future of high tech', *Technology Review*, 56, (6), pp. 18–21.

LEVINE, A. (1981) *Liberal Democracy: A Critique of its Theory*, New York: Macmillan.

LIGHTFOOT, S. (1973) 'Politics and reasoning: Through the eyes of teachers and children', *Harvard Educational Review*, 41, (2), pp. 197–244.

LINGARD, R. (1990) 'Corporate federalism: The emerging context of school policy-making in Australia'. Paper presented to the Australian Sociological Association, Brisbane, December 1990.

LINGARD, R. (1991) 'Policy-making for Australian schooling: The new corporate federalism', *Journal of Education Policy*, 6, (1), pp. 85–90.

LINGARD, R., KNIGHT, J., and PORTER, P. (Eds) (1993) *Schooling Reform in Hard Times*, London: Falmer Press.

LOUGH, N. *et al* (1990) *Today's Schools: A Review of the Education Reform Implementation Process*, Wellington: New Zealand Government Printer.

LOVEDAY, P. (1984) 'Corporatist trends in Australia', *Politics*, 1, pp. 46–51.

McCULLOCH, G. and NICHOLLS, J. (1987) 'Privatisation: A critical perspective', *Australian Universities' Review*, 30, (2), pp. 18–28.

McDONALD, E.D. (Ed.) (1961) *Phoenix: The Posthumous Papers of D.H. Lawrence*, London: Heinemann.

McGREGOR, D. (1960) *The Human Side of Enterprise*, New York: McGraw-Hill.

McLENNAN, G. *et al* (1984) *State and Society in Contemporary Britain*, Cambridge: Polity Press.

McPHERSON, A. and WILLIAMS, J.D. (1987) 'Equalisation and improvement: Some effects of comprehensive reorganisation in Scotland', *Sociology*, 21, pp. 509–40.

McWILLIAM, E. (1987) 'The challenge of the New Right: It's liberty versus equality and to hell with fraternity', *Discourse*, 8, (1), pp. 61–76.

MANDEL, E. (1976) *Late Capitalism*, London: Verso.

MANNHEIM, K. (1966) *Ideology and Utopia*, London: Routledge and Kegan Paul.

MARQUAND, J. (1989) *The Sources of Economic Growth*, Brighton: Harvester/Wheatsheaf.

MARSHALL, J. and PETERS, M. (1990) 'Empowering teachers'; *Unicorn*, 16, (3), pp. 163–8.

MARTIN, J. (1985) *Reclaiming a Conversation: The Ideal of the Educated Woman*, New Haven: Yale University Press.

MARTIN, J. (1991) 'Devolution and decentralization', in BOSTON, J., MARTIN, J., PALLOT, J. and WALSH, P. (Eds) *Reshaping the State: New Zealand's Bureaucratic Revolution*, Auckland: Oxford University Press, pp. 268–96.

MARX, K. (1961) *Capital*, Vol. 1, Moscow: Progress Press.

MARX, K. (1969) *Theories of Surplus Value*, Part 1, Moscow: Progress Press.

MATTHEWS, J. (1986) 'The politics of the "Accord" ', in MCKNIGHT, D. (Ed.) *Moving Left: The Future of Socialism in Australia*, Sydney: Pluto Press.

MEISENHELDER, T. (1983) 'The ideology of professionalism in higher education', *Journal of Education*, 165, (3), pp. 295–307.

MERTON, R.K. (1949) *Social Theory and Social Structure*, New York: Free Press.

MIDDLETON, S., CODD, J. and JONES, A. (Eds) (1990) *New Zealand Education Policy Today*, Wellington: Allen and Unwin.

MILIBAND, R. (1969) *The State in Capitalist Society: An Analysis of the Western System of Power*, London: Widenfeld & Nicholson.

MILLS, C. (1951) *White Collar*, New York: Oxford University Press.

MOODIE, G. and ACOPIAN, J. (1988) 'New instrumentalism in higher education: Another axe being ground', *Australian Universities' Review*, 31, (1), pp. 60–5.

MORGAN, G. (1986) *Images of Organisations*, London: Sage.

MULLER, D. *et al* (Eds) (1987) *The Rise of the Modern Educational System*, Cambridge: Cambridge University Press.

MURPHY, R. (1988) *Social Closure: The Theory of Monopolization and Exclusion*, Oxford: Clarendon.

NASH, R. (1983) *Schools Can't Make Jobs*, Palmerston North: Dunmore Press.

NASH, R. (1989) 'Tomorrow's schools: State power and parent participation', *New Zealand Journal of Educational Studies*, 24, (2), pp. 113–38.

NATIONAL COMMISSION ON EXCELLENCE IN EDUCATION (1983) *A Nation at Risk: The Imperative for Educational Reform*, Washington DC: United States Government Printing Office.

NEILL, A.S. (1970) *Summerhill*, Harmondsworth: Penguin.

NEW ZEALAND TREASURY (1987) *Government Management: Brief to the Incoming Government; Vol. 2, Education issues*, Wellington: NZ Government Printer.

NEWMAN, O. (1981) *The Challenge of Corporatism*, London: Macmillan.

NORMAN, R. (1982) 'Does equality destroy liberty?', in GRAHAM, K. (Ed.) *Contemporary Political Philosophy: Radical Studies*, Cambridge: Cambridge University Press.

NUNN, T.P. (1921) *Education: Its Data and First Principles*, London: Edward Arnold.

NUTTALL, D. (1988) 'The implications of national curriculum assessment', *Educational Psychology*, 8, pp. 229–36.

NUTTALL, D. (1989) 'National assessment! Complacency or misinterpretation?', in LAWTON, D. (Ed) *The Education Reform Act: Choice and Control*, London: Hodder and Stoughton.

O'CONNOR, D. (1987) 'Technological change and the restructuring of the global economy in the post-war period', in BURKE, G. and RUMBERGER, R. (Eds) *The Future Impact of Technology on Work and Education*, London: Falmer Press.

O'CONNOR, J. (1973) *The Fiscal Crisis of the State*, New York: St Martin's Press.

O'CONNOR, J. (1984) *Accumulation Crisis*, Oxford: Blackwell.

O'CONNOR, J. (1987) *The Meaning of Crisis*, Oxford: Blackwell.

O'HEAR, A. (1988) *Who Teaches the Teachers?*, London: Social Affairs Unit.

OAKESHOTT, M. (1967) *Rationalism in Politics*, London: Methuen.

OECD (1987) *Structural Adjustment and Economic Performance*, Paris: OECD.

OECD (1989) *Schools and Quality: An International Report*, Paris: OECD.

OFFE, C. (1975) 'The theory of the capitalist state and the problem of policy formation,' in LINDBERG, L. *et al* (Eds) *Stress and Contradiction in Modern Capitalism*, Massachusetts: Lexington Books, pp. 125–44.

OFFE, C. (1984) *Contradictions of the Welfare State*, London: Hutchinson.

OFFE, C. (1985) *Disorganized Capitalism: Contemporary Transformations of Work and Politics*, Cambridge: Polity Press.

OFFE, C. and RONGE, V. (1981) 'Thesis on the theory of the state', in DALE, R., ESLAND, G., FERGUSSON R. and McDONALD, M. (Eds) *Education and the State*, London: Falmer Press.

OFFICE OF THE MINISTER OF EDUCATION (1988) *Report of the Working Group on Post Compulsory Education and Training* (The Hawke Report), Wellington: NZ Government Printer.

OMNI, M. and WINANT, H. (1986) *Radical Formation in the United States*, New York: Routledge and Kegan Paul.

OZGA, J. (Ed.) (1988) *Schoolwork: Approaches To The Labour Process of Teaching*, Milton Keynes: Open University Press.

OZGA, J., and LAWN, M. (1981) *Teachers, Professionalism and Class*, London: Falmer Press.

PETERS, M. and MARSHALL, J. (1988) 'The politics of "Choice" and "Community"', *Access*, 7, pp. 94–106.

PETERS, R.S. (1966) *Ethics and Education*, London: Allen and Unwin.

PETERSON, A.D.C. (1960) *Arts and Science Sides in the Sixth Form*, Gulbenkian Foundation Report, Oxford University Department of Education.

PHENIX, P.H. (1964) *Realms of Meaning*, New York: McGraw Hill.

PICOT, B. (1988) *Administering For Excellence: Effective Administration in Education; Report of the Taskforce to Review Education Administration*, Wellington: NZ Government Printer.

PIERSON, C. (1986) *Marxist Theory and Democratic Politics*, Cambridge: Polity Press.

POPKEWITZ, T. (Ed.) (1987) *Critical Studies in Teacher Education: It's Folklore, Theory, and Practices*, London: Falmer Press.

POPKEWITZ, T. (1988) 'Educational reform: Rhetoric, ritual and social interest', *Educational Theory*, 38, (1), pp. 77–93.

PRESTON, N. (1989) 'The Dawkins *et al* managerial assessment push', *Education Links*, 35, pp. 21–3.

PUSEY, M. (1991) *Economic Rationalism in Canberra: A Nation Building State Changes Its Mind*, Cambridge: Cambridge University Press.

QUICKE, J. (1988) 'The "New Right" and education', *British Journal of Educational Studies*, 26, (1), pp. 5–20.

READ, H. (1964) *Art and Education*, Melbourne: F.W.Cheshire.

REID, L.A. (1961) *Ways of Knowledge and Experience*, London: Allen and Unwin.

REIMER, E. (1971) *School is Dead*, Harmondsworth: Penguin.

RENWICK, W.L. (Ed.) (1986) *Moving Targets: Six Essays on Educational Policy*, Wellington: New Zealand Council for Educational Research.

RICE, A. (1983) 'After bureaucracy, what?', *Urban Education*, 18, (1), pp. 40–58.

RIZVI, F. (1990) 'Horizontal accountability,' in CHAPMAN, J. (Ed.) *School-based Decision-making and Management*. London: Falmer Press, pp. 299–324.

RIZVI, F. and ANGUS, L. (1990) 'Reforming bureaucracy: An experiment in responsive educational governance', in CHAPMAN, J. and DUNSTAN, J. (Eds) *Bureaucracy and Democracy: Tensions in Public Schooling*, London: Falmer Press.

ROBERTSON, S. and WOOCK, R. (1989) 'Reform and reaction in Australian education', *Urban education*, 24, (1), pp. 3–24.

RUTTER, M. *et al* (1979) *Fifteen Thousand Hours: Secondary Schools and Their Effects on Children*, Shepton Mallet: Open Books.

RYAN, W. (1971) *Blaming the Victim*, New York: Pantheon.

SABEL, C.F. (1982) *Work and Politics*, Cambridge: Cambridge University Press.

SALTER, B. and TAPPER, T. (1981) *Education, Politics and the State*, London: Grant McIntyre.

SARASON, S. (1971) *The Culture of the School and the Problem of Change*, New York: Allyn and Bacon.

SAUSSURE, F. (1974) *Course in General Linguistics*, London: Fontana Books.

SCASE, R. and GOFFEE, R. (1989) *Reluctant Managers*, London: Unwin Hyman.

SCHÖN, D. (1983) *The Reflective Practitioner: How Professionals Think in Action*, New York: Basic Books.

SCHÖN, D. (1987) *Educating the Reflective Practitioner*, London: Jossey-Bass.

SCOTT, B. (1989) *Schools Renewal, Report of the Management Review Committee*, Sydney: NSW Education Portfolio.

SCRUTON, R. (1984) *The Meaning of Conservatism*, London: Macmillan.

SECADA, W. (Ed.) (1989) *Equity in Education*, London: Falmer Press.

SEDDON, T., ANGUS, L. and POOLE, M. (1990) 'Pressures on the move to school-based decision-making and management', in CHAPMAN, J. (Ed.) *School-based Decision-making and Management*, London: Falmer Press, pp. 29–54.

SELF, P. (1985) *Political theories of Modern Government: Its Role and Reform*, London: Allen and Unwin.

SHAW, R. (1992) *Teacher Training in Secondary Schools*, London: Kogan Page.

SHOR, I. (1980) *Critical Teaching and Everyday Life*, Boston: South End Press.

SHOR, I. (1986a) *Culture Wars: School and Society in the Conservative Restoration 1969–84*, New York: Routledge and Kegan Paul.

SHOR, I. (1986b) 'Equality is excellence: Transforming teacher education and the learning process', *Harvard Educational Review*, 56, (4), pp. 406–26.

SHOR, I. and FREIRE, P. (1987) *A Pedagogy for Liberation: Dialogues on Transforming Education*, South Hadley: Bergin & Garvey.

SHUKER, R. (1987) *The One Best System? A Revisionist History of State Schooling in New Zealand*, Palmerston North: Dunmore Press.

SIKES, P. *et al* (1985) *Teacher Careers: Crises and Continuities*, London: Falmer Press.

SIMON, R. (1982) *Gramsci's Political Thought*, London: Lawrence and Wishart.

SIMON, R. (1983) 'But who will let you do it? Counter hegemonic possibilities for work education', *Journal of Education*, 165, (3), pp. 235–56.

SLAUGHTER, S. (1985) 'The pedagogy of profit', *Higher Education*, 14, pp. 217–22.

SMITH, R. (1987) 'Becoming more self-reflexive in educational research', *Australian Educational Researcher*, 14, (3), pp. 47–56.

SMITH, R. (1992) 'Theory: An entitlement to understanding', *Cambridge Journal of Education*, 22, (3), pp. 387–98.

SMITH, R. and ZANTIOTIS, A. (1989) 'Practical teacher education and the *avante garde*, in GIROUX, H. and MCLAREN, P. (Eds) *Critical Pedagogy, the State and Cultural Struggle*, Albany: SUNY Press.

SMYTH, J. (1984a) 'Toward a "critical consciousness" in the instructional supervision of experienced teachers', *Curriculum Inquiry*, 14, (4), pp. 425–36.

SMYTH, J. (1984b) *Clinical Supervision — Collaborative Learning About Teaching: A Handbook*, Geelong: Deakin University Press.

SMYTH, J. (1985) 'Developing a critical practice of clinical supervision', *Journal of Curriculum Studies*, 17, (1), pp. 1–15.

SMYTH, J. (1986a) 'Towards a collaborative, reflective and critical mode of clinical supervision', in SMYTH, J. (Ed.) *Learning about Teaching Through Clinical Supervision*, London: Croom Helm.

SMYTH, J. (1986b) 'Clinical supervision: Technocratic mindedness, or emancipatory learning?', *Journal of Curriculum and Supervision*, 1, (4), pp. 331–40.

SMYTH, J. (1987a) 'Teachers-as-intellectuals in a critical pedagogy of schooling', *Education and Society*, 5, (1&2), pp. 11–28.

SMYTH, J. (1987b) *Rationale for Teachers' Critical Pedagogy: A Handbook*, Geelong: Deakin University Press.

SMYTH, J. (1989) 'A critical pedagogy of classroom practice', *Journal of Curriculum Studies*, 21, (6), pp. 483–502.

SMYTH, J. and GARMAN, N. (1989) 'Supervision as school reform: A critical perspective', *Journal of Education Policy* 4, (4), pp. 343–61.

SNOOK, I. (1989) 'Tomorrow's schools: Where are we now?', *The Sunday Supplement*, 12 November.

SNOOK, I. (1992) 'Teacher education: A sympathetic appraisal', Keynote Address to 'Teacher Education: An Investment For New Zealand's Future' Conference; Auckland, June.

SPENCER, H. (1963) *Essays on Education*, London: J.M. Dent and Sons.

STEVENS, P. (1987) 'Political education and political teachers', *Journal of Philosophy of Education*, 21, (1), pp. 75–83.

STILWELL, F. (1989) 'Economic rationalism is irrational', *Arena*, 87, pp. 139–45.

STRIKE, K. (1985) 'Is there a conflict between equity and excellence?', *Educational Evaluation and Policy Analysis*, 7, (4), pp. 405–16.

Sunkel, O. and Fuenzal, E. (1979) 'Transnationalization and its national consequences', in Villamil, J. (Ed.), *Transnational Capitalism and National Development*, Sussex: Harvester Press.

Super, R. (Ed.) (1962) *The Complete Prose Works of Matthew Arnold*, Ann Arbor: University of Michigan Press.

Therborn, G. (1980) *What Does the Ruling Class Do When It Rules?*, London: Verso.

Therborn, G. (1985) *Why are Some People More Unemployed than Others?*, London: Verso.

Thomas, J.B. (Ed.) (1990) *British universities and teacher education*, London: Falmer Press.

Torres, C. (1989) 'The capitalist state and public policy formation: Framework for a political sociology of educational policy making', *British Journal of Sociology of Education*, 10, (1), pp. 81–102.

Tucker, R.C. (1972) *The Marx-Engels Reader*, New York: W.W. Norton.

Urry, J. (1981) *The Anatomy of Capitalist Societies*, London: Macmillan.

Walker, J. (1980) 'The end of dialogue: Paulo Freire on politics and education' in Mackie, R. (Ed.) *Literacy and Revolution: The Pedagogy of Paulo Freire*, London: Pluto Press, pp. 120–50.

Walker, J. (1988) *Louts and Legends*, Sydney: Allen and Unwin.

Walker, J. (1990a) 'Policy directions in teacher education', *Unicorn*, 16, (3), pp. 142–7.

Walker, J. (1990b) 'Functional decentralisation and democratic control' in Chapman, J., (Ed.) *School-based Decision-making and Management*, London: Falmer Press, pp. 83–100.

Walker, S. and Barton, L. (Eds) (1987) *Changing Policies, Changing Teachers*, Milton Keynes: Open University Press.

Wallace, G. (Ed.) (1992) *Local Management of Schools: Research and Experience* (BERA Dialogues, No. 6), Clevedon: Longdunn Press.

Wallerstein, I. (1979) *The Capitalist World Economy*, Cambridge: Cambridge University Press.

Watkins, P. (1985) *Technology, the Economy and Education*, Geelong: Deakin University Press.

Watts, A.G. (1983) *Education, Unemployment and the Future of Work*, Milton Keynes: Open University Press.

Weiner, G. (1989) 'Feminism, equal opportunities and vocationalism: the changing context', in Burchell, H., and Millman, V. (Eds) *Changing Perspectives on Gender*, Milton Keynes: Open University Press.

Wexler, P. and Grabiner, G. (1986) 'The education question: America during the crisis', in Sharp, R. (Ed.) *Capitalist Crisis and Schooling: Comparative Studies in the Politics of Education*, Melbourne: Macmillan, pp. 1–40.

WHITE, J. (1988) 'Two national curricula — Baker's and Stalin's. Towards a liberal alternative', *British Journal of Educational Studies*, XXXVI, (3), pp. 218–31.

WHITEHEAD; A.N. (1929) *The Aims of Education*, New York: Williams and Norgate.

WHITTY, G. (1990) 'The New Right and the National Curriculum: State control or market forces?', in FLUDE, M., and HAMMER, M. (Eds) *The Education Reform Act, 1988: Its Origins and Implications*, London: Falmer Press.

WHITTY, G. (1991) *Next In Line For The Treatment? Education Reform and Teacher Education in the 1990's*, Inaugural Professorial Lecture, Goldsmiths' College, University of London.

WHITTY, G. (1992) *Education, Economy and National Culture*, Milton Keynes: Open University Press.

WHITTY, G. and MENTER, I. (1989) 'Lessons of Thatcherism: Education policy in England and Wales 1979–88', in GAMBLE, A. and WELLS, C. (Eds) *Thatcher's Law*, Wales: University of Wales Press.

WILDE, O. (1970) 'The soul of man under socialism' in *Complete Works of Oscar Wilde*, London: Collins.

WILKIN, M. (Ed.) (1992) *Mentoring in Schools*, London: Kogan Page.

WILLIAMS, R. (1963) *Culture and Society*, Harmondsworth: Penguin.

WILLIS, P. (1977) *Learning To Labour*, Farnborough: Saxon House.

WISE, A. (1979) *Legislated Learning: the Bureaucratization of the American Classroom*, Berkeley: University of California Press.

WOLFE, A. (1977) *The Limits of Legitimacy: Political Contradictions of Late Capitalism*, New York: Free Press.

WRIGHT, E.O. (1979) 'Intellectuals and the class structure of capitalist society', in WALKER, P. (Ed.) *Between Labor and Capital*, Boston: South End Press, pp. 191–211.

WRIGHT, N. (1983) 'Standards and the Black Papers', in COSIN, B. and HALES, M. (Eds) *Education, Policy and Society*, London: Routledge.

YEATMAN, A. (1990) *Bureaucrats, Technocrats, Femocrats: Essays on the Contemporary Australian State*, Sydney: Allen and Unwin.

YEATMAN, A. (1991) 'Corporate managerialism: An overview'. Paper presented to the NSW Teachers Federation Conference, The Management of Public Education, March 1991.

Index